White Magic Spell Book

A Modern Step-by-Step Guide to Light Spells, Love Magic, Divination and Rituals for a Better Life

Alysia Green

Table of Contents

Introduction

Greetings on the Road of Light! In this journey, you are setting forth into a realm that transcends our physical world, reaching into the essence of life, energy, and the very fabric of the universe itself. The enchantment you'll uncover in the coming pages isn't just fanciful imagination or mere illusion. Rather, it's a deeply spiritual discipline, grounded in the conviction that we have the power to consciously mold and direct energy to realize our aspirations and ambitions.

White magic, as you'll find, is a benevolent entity, focusing on healing, safeguarding, love, prosperity, and personal advancement. It's not a route for those seeking dominance over others or wishing to control the world according to their caprices. Instead, it's a journey for those in quest of the universe's harmony, personal enlightenment, and those desiring to make a positive impact on our world.

In this guide, we'll explore the many aspects of white magic, from grasping fundamental principles to delving into the intricacies of spell casting, botanic wisdom, crystal magic, lunar magic, divination, and more. You will receive guidance in establishing your holy sanctuary, nurturing your intuition, and learning to interact with the omnipresent energy.

Magic isn't about achieving immediate results or finding an easy path to success, but rather about transformation— within ourselves and our environment. It's a dedication to self-exploration, growth, and the manifestation of our most authentic and profound selves.

So, as you proceed through these pages, I encourage you to do so with receptiveness and an open mind. Let your spirit resonate with the wisdom encapsulated in these texts and allow your intuition to navigate this route.

Let the magic begin!

Chapter One: Origins and Foundations

White magic, in its most general interpretation, pertains to the harnessing of mystical forces or magic for altruistic ends. Yet, as one ventures further into the topic, it becomes clear that the essence of white magic is significantly more intricate and profound. Over the course of history, the notion of white magic has captivated human thought, materializing in a variety of manifestations across diverse cultures and epochs.

The origins of white magic are intertwined with the roots of humanity itself. We find evidence of magical practices in the earliest human societies. Primitive cave paintings depict scenes of ritual healing and successful hunting enchantments, while ancient sacred texts from Egypt and Babylonia are teeming with references to magical practices.

The concept of white magic, specifically, has been shaped significantly by ethical and religious perspectives. In stark contrast to black magic, which is associated with malevolent intent, white magic has always been viewed as a force for good. This is not to suggest that white magic is a means of realizing self-centered wishes. Instead, it is seen as a spiritual practice that encourages the practitioner to harmonize with the natural world, foster growth, heal, protect, and manifest positive changes.

The significance of white magic can be perceived not only in the acts it influences but also in the spiritual growth it fosters. Its practice entails a profound understanding of nature, its cycles, and the interconnectedness of all things. As such, the pursuit of white magic is not just a quest for power; it is a spiritual journey.

This way centers on harnessing the universal life force or energy that flows through everything. The practitioner of white magic learns to tap into this energy, channel it, and use it to bring about positive change. White magic, then, is not merely a set of spells or enchantments; it is a transformative practice, a path of wisdom, and an exercise in compassion.

Throughout the centuries, white magic has endured periods of misunderstanding and stigmatization, often being mistakenly associated with its darker counterpart. However, its enduring presence and continuous evolution are a testament to its timeless appeal and relevance. In the contemporary era, there has been a notable resurgence in the practice of white magic, fueled by a growing interest in alternative spirituality, embracing natural living, and seeking holistic healing.

At its heart, white magic is a recognition of the extraordinary within the commonplace, appreciating the inherent enchantment found in our daily existence. It acts as a subtle nudge, reminding us of our inborn ability to sculpt our realities, promote healing within ourselves and others, and inspire positive shifts in our personal spheres and the broader world. Its extensive lineage serves as a testament to the resilience of the undying human spirit and its relentless quest for wisdom, personal development, and peaceful coexistence.

Types of Magic and the Differences Between Them

The magic world is as diverse and complex as the world we inhabit daily, encompassing various branches, forms, and practices. Among the multitudes, white magic stands out, distinguished by its ethics, intention, and application. To understand these distinctions clearly, it's essential to compare and contrast white magic with other forms of magic.

The principal distinction between white magic and other forms of magic lies in the intent behind the practice. White magic is defined by the fundamental ethos of doing good – to help, to heal, and to protect. The magic is aimed at creating positive change without causing harm to anyone. This principle is guided by the Wiccan Rede, "An it harm none, do what ye will," which is widely accepted among white magic practitioners.

On the other hand, black magic is often associated with malevolent intentions, involving practices that aim to harm others or bend their will. It is seen as a tool for personal gain at the expense of others, breaking the universal law of free will. These stark differences in intent establish a clear boundary between white and black magic.

Grey magic is another term you might encounter, which refers to magic that blurs the line between black and white. Grey magic acknowledges that the world isn't merely binary and that intentions can often fall into a gray area. While grey magic doesn't seek to harm, it may sometimes prioritize the caster's needs or desires over the universal rule of non-harm, unlike white magic.

Another form of magic similar to white magic is green magic, also known as natural magic. This branch primarily focuses on the energies derived from the Earth and nature, like herbs, crystals, and elements. While white magic also utilizes these elements, it is broader in its practices and includes the ethical, spiritual, and healing aspects.

High and low magic, also known as ceremonial and folk magic, represent different approaches rather than different moralities. High magic is characterized by formal, elaborate rituals and ceremonies and often involves invoking higher beings. Low magic, in contrast, is simpler, drawing on everyday objects and actions to create change. White magic can be found in both high and low magic, depending on the nature of the rituals and the intent behind them.

Lastly, chaos magic, a relatively modern form of magic, is often seen as distinct from other forms due to its highly individualistic approach. Chaos magicians use whatever systems, beliefs, or practices work for them, emphasizing the efficacy of belief itself as a tool for change. While some chaos magicians might use methods similar to those found in white magic, they might not adhere to the same ethical guidelines.

While there are overlaps in methods and practices, the distinguishing factor of white magic is its commitment to positive intent, the healing and well-being of all, and adherence to a code of ethics that respects free will and causes no harm. This emphasis on intent and ethics makes white magic a uniquely nurturing and positive path within the vast and diverse world of magic.

Ethical Considerations in White Magic Practice

In practicing white magic, ethics play an integral role, shaping not only the manner of practice but also the very essence of it. As practitioners of white magic, we need to deeply understand and respect these ethical considerations, as they ensure that our practices align with the fundamental principles of harmlessness, respect for free will, and overall benevolence.

Principle of Harmlessness

When casting spells or conducting any magical work, we must ensure that our intentions and actions do not cause harm. For instance, a love spell aimed at making a specific person fall in love with you may seem harmless from your perspective, but it infringes on the other person's free will, effectively causing harm.

Respect for Free Will

Every individual has the right to exercise their free will, and this is a sacred principle within white magic. Manipulating or infringing upon someone's free will, even with seemingly benign intentions, is considered unethical. This means we cannot cast spells to change another person's behavior, thoughts, or feelings without their explicit consent. Instead, white magic encourages focusing on self-improvement and fostering positive change from within, which can indirectly affect your environment and relationships.

Principle of Responsibility

White magic also teaches the principle of personal responsibility, echoed in the Law of Threefold Return, which states that whatever energy one puts out into the world, whether good or bad, will return to them threefold. This principle encourages practitioners to think carefully about their intentions and actions, underscoring the importance of maintaining positivity and integrity in one's magical practices.

Respect for Nature

White magic encourages a deep respect for nature and all living beings, seeing the divine in every aspect of the natural world. As practitioners, we are stewards of the earth, and our magical practices should reflect this role. This means we strive to use sustainable and ethically sourced materials and to conduct rituals and spells in a way that honors and preserves nature.

Consent

Finally, even in healing or protection spells for others, consent is crucial. Regardless of our good intentions, performing magic on someone else's behalf without their knowledge or consent is seen as an infringement of their personal boundaries and free will.

Energy: The Basis of All Magic

The universe we inhabit is composed of energy. From the grandeur of galaxies to the smallest subatomic particles, everything we perceive and beyond is a manifestation of this energy in various forms. In white magic, this energy is the fundamental building block, the very basis of all magical practice.

Einstein's famous equation, $E=mc^2$, explains that matter and energy are interchangeable; they are different forms of the same fundamental substance. This concept is central to understanding energy within the realm of white magic. Every object, every living thing, and even thoughts and emotions consist of this energy, vibrating at different frequencies.

Understanding this allows us to grasp the underpinnings of magic. When we cast spells or perform rituals in white magic, we are essentially interacting with this universal energy. We are shaping, directing, or attracting it in ways that align with our intentions.

But what does energy feel like? How do we interact with it? Energy can manifest in various forms: as light, heat, motion, gravitational pull, electrical and magnetic forces, even our thoughts and emotions. You might feel it as a tingling sensation in your hands when you're channeling energy, or as a sense of warmth or coolness. It might be a gut feeling about a person or place, or an inexplicable connection to an object.

Psychic energy, particularly, plays a crucial role in white magic. This energy, which emanates from our thoughts and emotions, can influence the energies around us. This is why a clear, focused intention is so important in spell work. When we imbue our spells with positive and strong psychic energy, we can effectively manifest our desires.

Just as important as understanding energy is learning how to manage it. Grounding and centering are key techniques to stabilize our energies and connect with the energies of the Earth and the universe. Regular practices such as meditation, mindfulness, and chakra balancing can help us become more attuned to our own energy and the energies around us.

Cleansing and shielding are also vital in managing energy, helping us keep our energies pure and protected from negativity. Tools such as crystals, herbs, and sigils can aid us in these processes, each possessing unique energetic properties.

Understanding energy is not merely an intellectual exercise; it is an experiential journey. The more we work with energy, the more attuned we become to its nuances. As we deepen our relationship with energy, we expand our perception and enhance our magical abilities. It is the raw, dynamic force that we shape and direct in our magical work. By understanding and harnessing this energy, we can effect positive changes in ourselves and the world around us – the ultimate goal of white magic.

Symbols and Sigils

Symbols and sigils play a vital role in the practice of white magic, acting as focal points for harnessing and directing energy, representing intentions, and connecting with higher realms. They are powerful tools that can amplify our magical workings and deepen our spiritual connections.

Understanding Symbols

Symbols are signs, images, or objects that represent an idea, a concept, or a reality beyond their immediate, literal meaning. They hold immense power because they communicate on the level of the subconscious, speaking the language of the universal mind. In white magic, symbols serve as conduits, connecting the physical and spiritual realms and aiding the practitioner in invoking energies and beings from other dimensions.

A well-known example of a magical symbol is the pentagram, a five-pointed star enclosed in a circle, often used in Wiccan and Pagan practices. Each point of the star symbolizes one of the five elements – Earth, Air, Fire, Water, and Spirit, representing the interconnectedness of all life.

The Power of Sigils

A sigil, derived from the Latin word sigillum meaning seal, is a symbol created for a specific magical purpose. It is a pictorial representation of an intention or desire, designed to bypass the conscious mind and interact directly with the subconscious.

Creating a sigil involves focusing on your intention, then reducing this intention to a single statement. This statement is then converted into a symbolic representation through a process of simplification and combination of letters. The resulting image, unique and charged with your intention, is the sigil.

Role in White Magic

In white magic, symbols and sigils are used extensively in rituals and spellwork. They are drawn in the air with a wand or athame during the casting of a circle, inscribed on candles or written on paper during spellwork, or used in the creation of talismans and amulets.

Symbols and sigils act as a language to communicate our intentions to the universe, turning abstract thoughts into a tangible form. They can also serve as a bridge to connect us with specific energies, deities, or spiritual entities.

Moreover, symbols and sigils can be used for protection. Symbols of protection, like the triquetra or the eye of Horus, have been used across different cultures and eras. Sigils created for protection can be drawn on entrances to homes, carried in pockets, or even visualized as shields around us.

The act of creating a sigil is a magical act in itself, focusing and concentrating your intention through the process. Once created, the sigil is often activated or charged through concentration, visualization, or ritual, infusing it with energy before it is released into the universe to manifest your intention.

Understanding and working with symbols and sigils is a fascinating aspect of white magic. They form a powerful language of the subconscious, capable of conveying our deepest desires and highest intentions. With practice, they become a natural part of our magical toolkit, enhancing our ability to manifest and connect with the magical world around us.

Fundamental Ritual Tools in White Magic

Tools play an essential role in white magic, providing a physical medium through which practitioners can focus and direct their energies. Each tool carries a specific symbolic meaning and corresponds with certain elements, helping to create a balanced energetic environment for performing rituals and casting spells. Here, we will explore some of the fundamental ritual tools used in white magic.

Athame

The athame is a ceremonial knife, usually with a black handle, used in various magical practices. It represents the element of air and the power of the mind and intellect. It's important to note that the athame is not typically used for cutting in the physical sense, but for directing energy, casting the magic circle, and cutting through spiritual barriers.

Wand

The wand is a tool of invocation and is associated with the element of fire. It is used to focus and direct magical energy, invoke the quarters, and charge objects with magical intention. It symbolizes will, passion, transformation, and growth.

Chalice

The chalice or cup represents the element of water, associated with emotions, intuition, and the subconscious mind. It is often used to hold water or wine in rituals and symbolizes receptivity, mystery, and the divine feminine.

Pentacle

A pentacle is a disc or plate, often made of metal or clay, inscribed with a pentagram (a five-pointed star). It corresponds to the element of earth and symbolizes stability, manifestation, and the physical world. It is used to consecrate ritual tools, as a protective symbol, and to manifest intentions into the physical realm.

Altar

The altar is a dedicated space where practitioners place their ritual tools and other symbolic items. It serves as a focal point for rituals, a meeting place between the physical and spiritual realms. The arrangement of tools and items on the altar often reflects the personal beliefs and intentions of the practitioner.

Book of Shadows

The Book of Shadows is a personal magical journal where practitioners record their spells, rituals, magical experiences, and thoughts. It serves as a repository of wisdom, a record of one's magical journey.

Candles

Candles serve multiple purposes in white magic. Different colors are used to represent various intentions, elements, or deities. Candle magic is a significant aspect of white magic, where the candle's flame is seen as a beacon for manifesting intentions.

Crystals

Crystals are prized for their unique energetic properties. Each type of crystal holds a specific vibration that can be used to enhance rituals, spells, and healing practices. They can serve as tools for protection, energy amplification, and attuning to higher frequencies.

Incense and Herbs

Incense and herbs are used for cleansing, purifying, and creating sacred space. The specific type used depends on the intention of the ritual or spell. For example, sage is often used for smudging and clearing negative energy, while frankincense is used for purification and spiritual elevation.

While these tools can enhance your magical workings, the most potent tool is your intention and will. The magic lies within you; these tools simply help you to focus and direct it more efficiently.

Sacred Spaces: Altars, Temples, and Circles

In the practice of white magic, creating a sacred space is an essential step that helps us attune to the spiritual realms and focus our intentions. Sacred spaces serve as physical representations of the spiritual world and the boundaries between the two, acting as a conduit for magical energies. These spaces, like altars, temples, and circles, are sanctuaries where we can connect deeply with our inner selves, the divine, and the universe.

Altars

An altar is a personal and sacred area dedicated to magical workings, meditation, and spiritual practices. It's a place where practitioners can focus their intentions and manifest their desires. Altars are typically adorned with ritual tools, symbolic objects, and representations of the elements, deities, or spirits that resonate with the practitioner. The objects on the altar help concentrate energy and serve as focal points for visualization.

While there are traditional guidelines for setting up an altar, it is highly personal and should resonate with your beliefs and intentions. You may change your altar to reflect the seasons, your current focus, or different phases of your life.

Temples

In the realm of white magic, a temple need not be an elaborate, grandiose structure; instead, it could be any place sanctified for spiritual or magical pursuits. This might mean a special room within your house, a serene nook within your garden, or even a designated portion of your workspace. The integral feature of a temple lies in its distinction from common usage, coupled with the reverence and respect with which it is treated.

Your temple should be a place where you feel comfortable, safe, and empowered. This is a space where you'll perform rituals, meditate, and engage in other spiritual practices. It's a place that should be kept clean, serene, and infused with your intentions and positive energy.

Circles

The practice of casting a circle is a common feature in many magical traditions, including white magic. A circle is a sphere of energy constructed by the practitioner to create a sacred and protected space for conducting rituals and spellwork. It serves as a boundary between the world of the mundane and the world of the divine.

Casting a circle involves visualizing energy forming a sphere around your working space. This energy is often directed through a ritual tool, such as a wand or athame. The circle not only provides protection but also serves to contain and concentrate the energy raised during a ritual, enhancing the effectiveness of your magical workings.

Once the circle is cast, it becomes a sacred, otherworldly space where you can connect with higher realms, invoke deities or elemental forces, and focus your intentions for spellwork. After the ritual, the circle is usually closed, effectively returning the space to its normal state, with the energy raised during the ritual released or grounded.

Creating sacred spaces - altars, temples, and circles - is an act of reverence and devotion. These spaces help us focus our energies, define our intentions, and connect with the divine and the magic within us. They form an essential part of our journey in white magic, serving as physical reminders of our spiritual path and the transformational power of our intentions.

Chapter Two: Preparations as the Key to Success

The energy that we interact with and carry within us plays a significant role in our practices and experiences. Keeping our energetic bodies clean and protected is of utmost importance, not just for successful spellwork and rituals, but also for our overall well-being and spiritual growth. This chapter will explore the practices of energy cleansing and protection.

Energy Cleansing

Just as we cleanse our physical bodies, it's important to cleanse our energetic bodies, removing any negative or stagnant energy that we may have picked up. Energy cleansing can be done in several ways:

Smudging: This is a Native American practice that involves burning sacred herbs like sage, sweetgrass, or palo santo and using the smoke to cleanse a person, place, or object. The smoke is thought to carry away negative energies, leaving the space clear and purified.

Sound Therapy: Certain sounds can also cleanse energy. This could be achieved by using Tibetan singing bowls, bells, or tuning forks, or even by clapping or singing. The vibrations of these sounds disrupt and dispel negative energy.

Visualization: You can also cleanse your energy through visualization. Imagine a white or golden light washing over you, permeating your being, and flushing out any negative energies.

Crystals: Certain crystals, such as selenite and black tourmaline, are known for their cleansing properties. Placing these crystals in your space or carrying them with you can help keep your energy clean.

Energy Protection

After cleansing your energy, it's also important to protect it. Energy protection creates a barrier that shields you from external negative influences. Here are some ways to protect your energy:

Protection Symbols and Sigils: Certain symbols and sigils are known for their protective qualities. These can be drawn or visualized around you or your space for protection.

Crystals: Just as there are crystals for cleansing, there are also crystals for protection, such as black obsidian, amethyst, and labradorite.

Protection Spells and Rituals: There are numerous protection spells and rituals in white magic that you can perform, involving various tools like candles, herbs, and charms.

Visualizing Protective Shields: One common method of energy protection is to visualize a protective shield around you. This could be a bubble of white light, a mirrored sphere reflecting negativity, or even an armor of energy.

Effectiveness of energy cleansing and protection practices depends heavily on your intention and belief. It's important to approach these practices with respect, sincerity, and a clear mind. By regularly cleansing and protecting your energy, you're creating a harmonious environment for your magical workings and contributing to your personal and spiritual growth.

Balancing and Aligning Chakras

Within the realm of white magic, the practitioner's energy field, or aura, is of paramount importance. It is here that the seven main chakras reside, serving as focal points of spiritual power and transformation. By balancing and aligning these chakras, we can optimize our energy flow and enhance our magical practices.

The Chakras

The notion of chakras hails from the ancient spiritual customs of India. Each of the seven principal chakras aligns with a distinct region of the body and is linked with particular energies and facets of our existence. From the root chakra, situated at the spine's base, to the crown chakra at the pinnacle of the head, every chakra serves a singular purpose in our energetic.

1. Root Chakra (Muladhara): Represents our foundation and feeling of being grounded. It's associated with survival instincts and sense of security.

2. Sacral Chakra (Svadhisthana): Corresponds to creativity, sexuality, and our ability to accept new experiences.

3. Solar Plexus Chakra (Manipura): Represents personal power, willpower, and self-esteem.

4. Heart Chakra (Anahata): Symbolizes love, compassion, and emotional balance.

5. Throat Chakra (Vishuddha): Governs communication, self-expression, and truth.

6. Third Eye Chakra (Ajna): Corresponds to intuition, imagination, and wisdom.

7. Crown Chakra (Sahasrara): Represents spiritual connection, enlightenment, and universal consciousness.

Balancing and Aligning the Chakras

White magic provides us with a variety of tools and techniques to balance and align our chakras. Here are a few methods:

Meditation: Each chakra has its own seed mantra and corresponding visual symbol. By focusing on these during meditation, we can activate and harmonize the energy of each chakra. For example, visualizing a vibrant red lotus at the base of the spine while chanting 'LAM' can help balance the root chakra.

Crystal Healing: Different crystals resonate with different chakras. Placing the appropriate crystal on the corresponding chakra while lying down can aid in balancing that chakra's energy. For instance, a clear quartz crystal can be used for the crown chakra, while a rose quartz can be used for the heart chakra.

Aromatherapy and Herbs: Certain essential oils and herbs can also help balance the chakras. For example, sandalwood and frankincense can aid in opening the third eye, while lavender and chamomile can help calm the throat chakra.

Energy Healing: Practices like Reiki, Qi Gong, and Tai Chi work directly with the body's energy and can be very effective in balancing and aligning the chakras.

Balancing and aligning our chakras can greatly enhance our overall wellbeing and our magical practices. It helps us to become more attuned to our internal energy flow and the subtle energies around us, leading to greater harmony and effectiveness in our spellwork and rituals. Regular practice of chakra work will support a healthy, vibrant, and potent energy field, ready for the magical workings of white magic.

Listening to Your Inner Voice

Within the realm of white magic, intuition holds immense power. It's our internal counsel guiding us toward authenticity and enlightenment, a profound comprehension that transcends ordinary logic or conscious thought. Honing this inherent capability can considerably augment your magical pursuits, allowing you to become more receptive to surrounding energies and more perceptive in deciphering the indications and symbols within your magical practices.

Intuition

Intuition is often characterized as an instinctive feeling, a premonition, or an internal counsel. It represents our subconscious mind dialoguing with us, relying on a reservoir of information and experiences that our conscious mind may not fully perceive.

Within the practices of white magic, intuition can provide guidance in a plethora of ways. It can steer us towards the appropriate spell or ritual for a specific scenario, assist us in interpreting the outcomes of divination, or encourage us to undertake certain actions while evading others. It can also aid us in forging connections with spiritual beings, discern surrounding energies, and comprehend profound truths about ourselves and the cosmos.

Developing Your Intuition

Strengthening intuition is akin to training a muscle—the more frequently it's employed, the more robust it becomes. Here are some techniques to help you sync with your internal counsel:

Meditation: Routine meditation can assist in calming your mind, making it simpler for you to perceive your internal voice. You can practice mindfulness meditation to enhance your awareness of your thoughts and emotions, or you can engage in guided meditations specifically devised to bolster intuition.

Journaling: Documenting your thoughts, emotions, and dreams can assist in tapping into your subconscious mind and identifying intuitive revelations. Be particularly observant of recurring themes or symbols, as they might convey significant messages from your intuition.

Intuition Exercises: Practice listening to your intuition in everyday situations. For example, before checking the caller ID on a ringing phone, try to intuit who's calling. Or try intuiting what color shirt a friend will be wearing before you meet them. These exercises can help you trust and develop your intuition.

Nature Connection: Spending time in nature can help you attune to your intuition. Nature is full of subtle energies and messages, and by immersing yourself in it, you can learn to perceive these subtle signs and signals.

Dream Work: Our dreams can be a rich source of intuitive insights. Keeping a dream journal and learning to interpret your dreams can help you tap into this source of wisdom.

Divination Practices: Techniques such as tarot reading, rune casting, or scrying can also help you develop your intuition. These practices involve interpreting symbolic messages, which can hone your intuitive abilities.

Developing your intuition is a lifelong journey. It requires patience, trust, and open-mindedness. There may be times when your intuition seems vague or confusing, but with time and practice, it will become clearer and more reliable.

Your intuition is a unique and personal guide. It's there to help you navigate your magical practice and your life with greater wisdom and insight. Trust in it, listen to it, and let it illuminate your path in the world of white magic.

Chapter Three: The Elements in White Magic

In the realm of white magic, the components of Earth, Air, Fire, and Water are esteemed as foundational aspects of the cosmos. These elements symbolize different forms of energy and are deeply woven into our existence and magical operations. This section is dedicated to unraveling the roles and significance of these elements in the context of white magic.

The notion of these four elements springs from ancient philosophies and has found a home in various magical and spiritual paradigms, including white magic. Each element aligns with unique qualities, directions, hues, and symbols:

Earth: Symbolic of stability, grounding, and physical existence. It aligns with the North, the shade of green, and the pentacle emblem.

Air: Associated with intellect, dialogue, and transition. It links to the East, the color yellow, and the symbol of the sword.

Fire: Epitomizes passion, transformation, and determination. It relates to the South, the color red, and the wand insignia.

Water: Reflects emotions, intuition, and healing. It is linked with the West, the color blue, and the chalice symbol.

Let's delve into each element in more depth now.

Earth: Stability and Prosperity

The element of Earth holds a foundational place in the practice of white magic. Associated with the physical, Earth represents grounding, stability, abundance, and prosperity. As practitioners, understanding and harnessing the power of this element can greatly enhance our magical workings.

The Energy of Earth

Earth energy is the embodiment of groundedness, practicality, and endurance. It is the stabilizing force that nurtures life, the physical matter that makes up our world, and the silent energy that gives form and substance to our desires.

In the wheel of the year, Earth corresponds with the direction of North, the season of winter, and the time of midnight. It is symbolized by the color green or brown, the pentacle, and stones and crystals. In the human body, Earth is connected to the root chakra, grounding us in our physical existence.

Working with Earth Energy

Harnessing the energy of Earth in your white magic practices can enhance your work in many ways, particularly when you seek to manifest stability, abundance, and prosperity. Here are a few ways to engage with Earth energy:

Grounding Practices: Grounding is the process of connecting your energy with that of the Earth. This can be done through visualizations, such as imagining roots growing from your feet into the ground, or through physical activities, like walking barefoot in nature or gardening.

Crystals and Stones: Earth's energy can be accessed through crystals and stones. Use stones like green aventurine or citrine in your rituals to attract prosperity, or hematite and black tourmaline for grounding and protection.

Earth-based Rituals and Spells: Spells and rituals that involve burying objects, using herbs and plants, or that are designed to bring about physical manifestations are great ways to work with Earth energy.

Pentacle Work: The pentacle, a five-pointed star within a circle, is a symbol of Earth. It represents the four elements (Earth, Air, Fire, and Water) and Spirit, encompassed by the divine circle. Incorporate pentacles into your ritual work to draw on the energy of Earth.

Offerings to Earth Spirits: In many magical traditions, offerings are made to Earth spirits or deities associated with the Earth. This might include leaving food or drink offerings, or performing acts of service like planting trees or cleaning up natural areas.

The element of Earth is all about manifestation. It takes the ethereal and makes it tangible. Whether you seek to attract wealth, improve your health, create stability, or manifest a specific goal, the Earth element is a powerful ally in your white magic practice. As with all elements, approach Earth with respect, gratitude, and a clear intention, and you'll find it a sturdy foundation for your magical work.

Air: Communication and Inspiration

The element of Air holds a powerful role in the sphere of white magic. As the breath of life, it governs communication, inspiration, wisdom, and change. This chapter will help you understand the essence of Air and how to utilize its power in your magical workings.

The Essence of Air

Air, in the context of white magic, symbolizes the invisible, yet pervasive, forces of life. It is associated with the mind, intellect, and spirit. As we breathe in, Air sustains our physical life, and metaphorically, it fuels our intellectual and creative inspirations.

Air corresponds to the direction of East, the season of spring, and the dawn. Its color is often represented as yellow or light blue, and its symbol in ritual is the athame or sword. In the human body, Air resonates with the heart chakra and the process of respiration.

Working with Air Energy

Air is crucial in white magic, especially when the intention involves communication, intellectual pursuits, or creative inspiration. Here's how you can incorporate the energy of Air into your magical practice:

Breathing Practices: Breathwork is a powerful way to harness Air's energy. Conscious breathing can bring clarity, release energy blockages, and help attune you to the subtle forces of magic.

Writing and Speaking: As Air governs communication, the acts of writing and speaking are imbued with its power. Use written spells, incantations, and affirmations in your magic to bring about change and manifestation.

Feathers and Incense: Feathers symbolize Air's connection to birds and flight, while incense represents the visible aspect of Air. Use these tools in your rituals to represent and invoke the element of Air.

Wind Chimes and Bells: Sound is a manifestation of Air. The use of wind chimes or bells in your magical practice can help you tune into Air's frequency.

Air-based Rituals and Spells: Spells involving the mind, communication, travel, and inspiration benefit from the influence of Air. This can involve casting spells on a windy day, or using words and sounds as primary spell ingredients.

Offerings to Air Spirits: Leaving offerings to spirits or deities of the Air can help cultivate a relationship with this element. This might include leaving out feathers or burning incense in their honor.

Working with Air can significantly enhance your white magic practice. As the force that carries our intentions out into the universe, it is a key player in spellcasting and magical workings. By cultivating a relationship with Air, you can harness its power of transformation, wisdom, and communication to enhance your magic and enrich your life.

Fire: Passion and Transformation

Fire is a potent and dynamic element. It symbolizes passion, transformation, courage, and willpower. Understanding the nature of Fire and how to harness its energy can greatly enrich your magical practice.

The Essence of Fire

Fire represents the spark of life, the driving force behind movement and change. It is associated with passion, desire, and transformation. Fire is the element that turns our innermost wishes into reality and pushes us towards action and change.

In the wheel of the year, Fire corresponds to the direction of South, the season of summer, and the time of midday. Its symbolic color is red or orange, and it is represented by the wand or staff in rituals. Within the human body, Fire resonates with the solar plexus chakra, our center of personal power and determination.

Working with Fire Energy

Harnessing Fire energy in your magical workings can lend power to your intentions, particularly those involving transformation, courage, and passion. Here are some methods to engage with Fire energy:

Candle Magic: Fire is often invoked in candle magic. The act of lighting a candle can symbolize the bringing of light to darkness, the manifestation of your intentions, and the transformation of your desires into reality.

Bonfires and Hearth Fires: Larger fires, like bonfires or hearth fires, can be used in rituals and celebrations, particularly those that involve purification, transformation, or community connection.

Sun Magic: As the most significant source of natural fire, the Sun can be invoked in your spells and rituals. Sun magic can involve everything from simple dawn meditations to complex rituals performed at solar noon.

Fire-based Rituals and Spells: Spells that involve burning— whether it's a piece of paper with a written intention, a photograph, or a symbol—are a powerful way to utilize Fire energy.

Offerings to Fire Spirits: Offerings to deities or spirits associated with Fire can help you form a bond with this element. This might involve burning herbs, oils, or incense, or offering foods cooked over a fire.

Fire is a powerful force of change and transformation, but it is also a force to be respected. Always use Fire safely and responsibly in your magical practice. With careful use, Fire can help you burn away the old to make way for the new, fuel your passions, and transform your intentions into reality. Harness its energy with respect and care, and it will be a powerful ally in your white magic practice.

Water: Healing and Intuition

In the tradition of white magic, Water is a deeply nurturing and intuitive element. It symbolizes healing, emotions, and intuition, offering a wellspring of wisdom for those who connect with its energies. This chapter explores the nature of Water and its application in your magical practice.

The Essence of Water

Water is life-giving, soothing, and deeply mysterious. It is linked to our emotions, intuition, and the world of dreams. Just as physical water nurtures life and facilitates cleansing, the element of Water in a metaphysical sense aids in emotional healing, purifying negative energies, and enhancing psychic abilities.

Water corresponds to the direction of West, the season of autumn, and the twilight hours. It's represented by the color blue or silver, and its ritual symbol is the chalice or cup. Within the human body, Water resonates with the sacral chakra, the energy center connected to emotions and creativity.

Working with Water Energy

Incorporating the energy of Water into your magical practice can aid in emotional healing, enhance your intuition, and deepen your emotional connections. Here are ways to engage with Water energy:

Bathing and Washing Rituals: Water is commonly used in rituals of cleansing and purification. Ritual baths, for instance, can be used for personal purification, healing, or preparing for magical work.

Moon Magic: The moon, with its pull on the tides, is closely associated with the element of Water. Working with lunar cycles in your magic can help attune you to the ebb and flow of Water energy.

Dream Work: Water's association with intuition and the subconscious makes it an excellent ally in dream work. Keeping a dream journal and using dreams in your magical practice can help you tap into Water's intuitive wisdom.

Divination: Practices such as scrying in a bowl of water or reading tea leaves are ways to connect with Water's intuitive and psychic properties.

Water-based Rituals and Spells: Spells and rituals that involve the use of water, or that are designed to enhance intuition, healing, or emotional connection, can benefit from the influence of Water.

Offerings to Water Spirits: Offerings to deities or spirits of Water can help build a relationship with this element. This could include leaving out a bowl of fresh water, pouring libations, or offering shells or other tokens of the sea.

As you explore the energies of Water, remember to approach it with reverence and respect. The healing and intuitive powers of Water offer profound wisdom and assistance in your magical workings. Embrace its depths, and it will surely enrich your practice of white magic.

Chapter Four: Crystals in White Magic

Crystals play an integral role in the practice of white magic. Each crystal possesses unique energetic properties that can be harnessed for various purposes, from enhancing psychic abilities to promoting physical healing.

Crystals are not just beautiful stones; they are powerful tools brimming with natural energy. Each crystal resonates with specific frequencies that can influence our own energy fields. They can absorb, focus, direct, detoxify, shift, and diffuse energy within the body, helping to bring balance to our physical and emotional states.

Crystal magic refers to the use of crystals and gemstones as tools in magical workings. Each crystal carries specific vibrational frequencies, resonating with different energies and properties. Crystal magic is about attuning to these energies to enhance and manifest your intentions.

Principles of Crystal Magic

Using crystals in magic involves a few basic principles:

- Cleansing: Crystals often absorb energy from their surroundings. Regular cleansing ensures they're free from negative energies.

- Charging: After cleansing, crystals need to be recharged. This could be done by moonlight, sunlight, or burying them in the earth.

- Programming: To use a crystal for a specific purpose, you'll need to program it with your intention. This can be done through meditation or by simply holding the crystal and focusing on your intention.

- Application: The use of crystals varies widely. They can be worn as jewelry, placed around the home, used in meditation, incorporated into spells and rituals, or used in energy healing.

The key to effective crystal magic lies in your personal connection with your crystals. Trust your intuition as you work with these earth energies, and let the magic unfold.

Key Crystals for White Magic and Their Properties

Crystals play a vital role in white magic, each carrying specific vibrations that resonate with different aspects of our being. This chapter focuses on the key crystals commonly used in white magic and the properties they embody.

Clear Quartz: Clear Quartz, also known as the 'Master Healer,' holds a unique position in the realm of crystals due to its versatility and power. This translucent crystal is renowned for its ability to amplify energy and thought, making it a potent tool for intention-setting and manifestation. It can absorb, store, release, and regulate energy, which can help balance the chakras and harmonize the aura. Clear Quartz can also amplify the energies of other crystals, enhancing their effects when used together. Additionally, it's often utilized in spells and rituals of all kinds - from protection and healing to love and abundance. Due to its clear and neutral color, it can be charged with any intention and used in any spell or ritual, making it a staple in any crystal collection. The shape of Clear Quartz also influences its properties; for example, a Clear Quartz point directs energy, while a Clear Quartz cluster radiates energy in all directions.

Amethyst: Amethyst, with its mesmerizing purple hue, is one of the most spiritually resonant stones. It's known to stimulate the crown and third eye chakras, enhancing spiritual awareness, psychic abilities, and intuition. This makes it an excellent stone for meditation, helping to quiet the mind, deepen the meditative state, and open the gateway to higher consciousness. In addition, Amethyst carries strong protective energies. It's said to create a protective shield around its carrier, warding off negative energy, psychic attack, and harmful influences. This gemstone is also thought to purify the mind and clear it of negative thoughts, making it a natural tranquilizer that can help alleviate stress and anxiety. For these reasons, Amethyst can be used in rituals for protection, healing, spiritual growth, and peace.

Citrine: Known as a stone of light, joy, and abundance, Citrine embodies the energy of the sun. This bright yellow to golden crystal is most often associated with the solar plexus chakra, which is the center of willpower and confidence. Therefore, Citrine is often used in spells and rituals for prosperity and success, as it's believed to manifest abundance and bring good luck. It's also an excellent tool for boosting self-confidence, motivation, and personal power. As a revitalizing and cleansing stone, Citrine is also said to stimulate the mind, increasing concentration and promoting creativity. This makes Citrine a beneficial crystal for students and professionals who are looking for a boost in their work. Citrine is also one of the few crystals that never need cleansing as it does not hold or accumulate negative energy but dissipates and transmutes it.

Rose Quartz: Known as the 'Stone of Love', Rose Quartz resonates with the energy of unconditional love and infinite peace. Its soft, gentle pink hue mirrors its nurturing and comforting properties. This crystal opens the heart chakra, encouraging self-love, friendship, and deep inner healing. It's particularly effective in attracting romantic love or enhancing existing relationships, which makes it a favorite for love spells or rituals aimed at fostering forgiveness and compassion. Rose Quartz is also used for emotional healing, as it helps release unexpressed emotions and heartache, transforming emotional conditioning that no longer serves you. If you're working on self-esteem, self-trust, or self-worth, Rose Quartz can be a valuable ally.

Black Tourmaline: Black Tourmaline is often considered a powerful protective and grounding stone. It's deeply connected to the base chakras, grounding you firmly in the earth while creating a shield against negative energies. This crystal is often used in protection spells, especially those that aim to ward off negative energy, harmful thoughts, or psychic attacks. It's also believed to help turn negative thoughts into positive ones, providing emotional stability. Due to its grounding properties, Black Tourmaline can also be used to promote a connection with the physical world and to help you feel more centered and secure.

Selenite: Selenite, named after the Greek goddess of the moon, Selene, is a high vibration crystal that instills deep peace and is excellent for meditation or spiritual work. It's known for its brilliant radiance and is often used for clearing negative energy from the body, mind, and spirit, as well as from other crystals and environments. Selenite is believed to open the crown and higher chakras, helping to access angelic consciousness and higher guidance. It also promotes mental clarity, clearing confusion and revealing the bigger picture behind any problem. Therefore, Selenite can be a useful tool for spiritual development, aiding in the evolution of your consciousness and in accessing your inner wisdom.

Moonstone: Moonstone, with its ethereal glow, is deeply connected to lunar energy and the divine feminine. It's considered a stone of new beginnings and is believed to enhance intuition and empathy. Moonstone is particularly connected with the third eye and crown chakras, aiding in the development of psychic abilities and spiritual insights. Due to its strong ties to the moon, it's also frequently used for dream work, helping to facilitate lucid dreaming and dream recall. It's often used in spells related to the divine feminine, making it a popular choice for fertility and pregnancy spells. Additionally, Moonstone is known for its powerful emotional healing properties, helping to soothe and balance emotions, making it a useful tool in rituals and spells aimed at emotional wellbeing and harmony.

Lapis Lazuli: Known for its striking deep blue color, Lapis Lazuli has been treasured throughout history as a stone of wisdom and truth. It's connected primarily with the third eye chakra, promoting intellectual ability, enhancing memory, and encouraging a desire for knowledge. Lapis Lazuli encourages honesty of the spirit, and in the spoken and written word. It's also known to aid in the process of learning and is especially excellent for enhancing memory. Due to these properties, it's often used in spells for success in studies or to enhance intellectual abilities. In addition, Lapis Lazuli can facilitate self-awareness and self-expression, making it useful in spells for personal growth and understanding. This stone is also known to attract success, making it a powerful stone for enhancing career performance or any other area of life where you could use a boost.

While each crystal carries specific energies, your personal connection to the crystal also matters. Feel free to trust your intuition in choosing the right crystal for your needs. With a respectful approach and a clear intention, you can forge a powerful bond with these earthly treasures and deepen your white magic practice.

Cleansing, Charging, and Programming Crystals

When you start working with crystals, understanding the process of cleansing, charging, and programming them is vital. These practices ensure that your crystals are free of any previous energies and are attuned to your unique intentions.

Cleansing Crystals

Cleansing is the process of clearing your crystals of any previous energies they have absorbed. There are several ways to cleanse your crystals:

Smudging: This involves burning sacred herbs like sage or palo santo and passing your crystal through the smoke.

Sound: The vibrations from singing bowls, tuning forks, or even clapping or singing can also cleanse crystals.

Moonlight: Placing your crystals in moonlight overnight, especially during a full moon, can cleanse and recharge them.

Running Water: Natural running water, such as a river or stream, can cleanse crystals. Be aware that some crystals are sensitive to water and can be damaged by this method.

Charging Crystals

Charging your crystals means energizing them, and there are several methods to do this:

Sunlight/Moonlight: Leaving your crystals in sunlight or moonlight can energize them. However, be cautious, as some crystals can fade under prolonged sunlight.

Earth: Burying your crystals in the earth allows them to absorb natural energies, recharging them.

Using Larger Crystals: Larger crystals, like big quartz clusters or selenite slabs, can charge smaller crystals. Simply place the smaller crystal on the larger one overnight.

Programming Crystals

Programming a crystal involves setting a specific intention within the crystal. This intention directs the energy of the crystal in your magical work. To program your crystal:

Hold your crystal in your dominant hand (the one you write with).

Clear your mind and focus on your intention for the crystal. Visualize your intention as a beam of light moving from your mind, through your arm, and into the crystal.

Say your intention aloud if you wish, or hold it in your mind. Feel the energy of your intention charging the crystal.

Trust that your crystal is now programmed, and thank it for its assistance.

Your relationship with your crystals is personal. It's more important to listen to your intuition than to follow any specific rules. As you grow in your practice, you'll find the methods that work best for you.

Incorporating Crystals in Spell Work and Healing

Crystals, with their unique energies and properties, can be powerful allies in spell work and healing. This chapter will guide you on how to incorporate crystals into your magical and healing practices.

Crystals in Spell Work

In spell work, crystals can be used to amplify your intentions, connect with specific energies, and act as focal points for manifestation. Here are a few ways to incorporate crystals into your spells:

Intention Setting: When casting a spell, place a crystal that aligns with your intention on your altar or hold it in your hand to amplify your focus.

Crystal Grids: A crystal grid involves arranging multiple crystals in a geometric pattern to manifest a specific intention. The combined energies of the crystals, amplified by their arrangement, work to manifest your intention.

Wands: Some practitioners use crystal wands to direct energy in a spell. A wand can be used to cast a circle, draw symbols or sigils, or point towards an object to direct energy towards it.

Crystals in Healing

Crystals can also play a major role in energy healing practices, such as reiki, chakra balancing, or aura cleansing. Here's how you can use them:

Chakra Balancing: Each of the seven chakras corresponds to specific crystals. Placing the corresponding crystal on each chakra point can help align and balance your chakra system.

Aura Cleansing: You can cleanse your aura by sweeping a selenite wand around your body, visualizing it pulling away any negativity or energetic blockages.

Healing Layouts: Similar to crystal grids, healing layouts involve placing crystals on or around the body in specific patterns for physical or emotional healing.

Elixirs: Some crystals can be used to create gem elixirs or crystal-infused water. Always make sure the crystal is safe for immersion in water, and avoid toxic or friable stones.

The effectiveness of using crystals in spell work and healing depends heavily on your intention, focus, and belief in their power. Always cleanse and program your crystals before using them and trust your intuition when selecting crystals for your work. The more you work with your crystals, the more attuned to their energies you will become.

Chapter Five: Herbalism in White Magic

Herbs are deeply entwined with the practice of white magic, acting as conduits for the natural world's abundant energies. Just as every stone and crystal reverberates with its own unique energy, so too does every plant, flower, and herb.

The intrinsic link between herbs and white magic has its roots in the idea that all things in nature contain an inherent magical property. Herbs, due to their variety, accessibility, and strong association with earth's healing energies, have always played a significant role in this realm.

Historical Significance

The use of herbs in magic has a rich history, extending across many cultures and ages. Ancient civilizations utilized herbs in their religious ceremonies, healing practices, and rituals. From the shamans of indigenous tribes to the healers of Ancient Egypt, herbs were often used for their magical properties. Many of these traditions have carried forward into modern magical practices.

Therapeutic and Magical Properties

The potency of herbs in white magic comes from their dual role - their therapeutic and magical properties. For instance, lavender is not just therapeutically used for its calming effects; it is also used in spells for relaxation, peace, and love due to its harmonious vibrations. Each herb, in its essence, contains properties that align with specific intentions, making them dynamic tools in spell work and healing.

Symbolism and Correspondences

Each herb symbolizes a particular element, planet, or deity, offering further depth to its magical uses. These associations, often known as correspondences, can enhance your magical workings by aligning them with specific energies. For instance, rosemary is often associated with the sun and can be used in spells and rituals related to personal power, purification, and healing.

Methods of Using Herbs in White Magic

In white magic, herbs can be used in various ways. They can be incorporated into spell jars, sachets, or amulets for protection or attraction spells. In ritual work, herbs can be burnt as incense, added to ritual baths, or used to anoint candles. In healing, herbs might be used to create balms or teas. The flexibility and variety of herbs make them a staple in any magical practice.

Ethics and Sustainability

An important part of using herbs in white magic is approaching them with respect and a focus on sustainability. This means harvesting herbs responsibly, considering the health of the plant and its continued growth, and prioritizing the conservation of wild plant populations. The connection between the practitioner and nature is a vital part of white magic, and respectful interaction is at the heart of this relationship.

The importance of herbs in white magic cannot be overstated. They are a living, breathing aspect of nature, embodying earth's energy in a form that can be directly incorporated into magical practices. From their historical significance to their diverse uses, herbs provide a tangible and versatile way to connect with the magic that pulses through our natural world.

Most Common Herbs Used and Their Symbolism

The following are some of the most commonly used herbs in white magic, each with its symbolism that enriches its magical applications.

Rosemary

This fragrant herb, associated with the sun and the element of fire, is highly valued for its purification, protection, and healing properties. The vibrant energy of rosemary is believed to boost memory and mental clarity, making it an excellent tool for enhancing cognitive function and creativity. It has been used in love spells due to its association with fidelity, honesty, and love. When burned, rosemary releases its potent properties into the air, clearing negative energies and purifying your environment. This makes it a popular choice for cleansing rituals and a vital ingredient in protection spells. You might place rosemary at entrances to your home for protection or use it in a bath for a purifying cleanse. The herb's robust aroma also makes it a fantastic ingredient for creating sacred oils or incense.

Sage

Sage, with its strong connection to wisdom, purification, and protection, holds a revered place in various magical practices. It is linked to the element of air and often associated with the goddess Diana and the moon, symbolizing spiritual clarity, intuition, and a deeper connection to the divine. Its smoky, aromatic scent is well known for dispelling negative energy and bringing calmness when used in smudging rituals—a practice common in many Indigenous cultures and adopted in various forms by different spiritual communities. In such a ritual, a sage bundle is lit, and the smoke is gently wafted around a person or a space to cleanse the aura or environment. In healing rituals, sage can be used in baths or made into a tea. Sage's power of protection is often employed in warding off evil influences and creating a safe, sacred space for magic and meditation.

Lavender

Known for its soothing aroma and beautiful purple hue, lavender is a potent herb associated with Mercury and the element of air. In magical practices, it embodies tranquility, happiness, and love. Lavender is renowned for its calming properties; thus, it is often used in spells and rituals aimed at calming anxiety, soothing the mind, and promoting emotional balance. Its energy promotes harmony and peace, making it an ideal herb for healing rituals or for any work aimed at resolving conflicts. The herb's connection to love and affection also makes it popular in love spells, whether attracting new love or deepening existing relationships. As an ingredient in dream pillows, it may help encourage restful sleep and prophetic dreams.

Basil

Known for its rich, spicy scent, basil is linked with Mars and the element of fire. It carries strong energies of abundance, prosperity, and protection. In magic, it's often used in wealth and prosperity spells—carrying a basil leaf in your wallet or purse, or sprinkling some on your doorstep are traditional practices thought to attract money and success. Basil's protective properties can be employed in rituals for warding off negativity and evil; it's often hung in doorways or windows for this purpose. The herb's association with love and harmony makes it a powerful ingredient in spells to foster a happy home and encourage understanding and love within family and relationships. Basil can also be used in divination and is a popular ingredient in incense blends and herbal amulets.

Mint

Connected to Venus and the element of air, mint is a lively herb symbolizing vitality, communication, and abundance. Its bright, fresh scent reflects its invigorating energy and the stimulating effects it can have on the mind. Mint is frequently used in spells aimed at attracting money and success—keeping a few leaves in your wallet or using it in a money drawing oil are common practices. Its association with travel makes it a suitable ingredient in safe travel spells or charms. Additionally, mint's refreshing and communicative energy aids in enhancing mental alertness and breaking through communication barriers, making it a helpful tool in spells for clarity and eloquence.

Chamomile

Associated with the sun and linked to the element of water, chamomile is a gentle herb embodying healing, purification, and love. Its delicate, soothing aroma aligns with its calming properties—often used in spells to promote peace, tranquility, and restful sleep. Chamomile tea is a popular calming drink before sleep, and the herb is commonly used in sleep pillows or bath spells to promote relaxation and peaceful dreams. It's also employed to attract good fortune and prosperity, often carried in a charm bag or used in washes for money drawing purposes. Furthermore, chamomile can be used in purification rituals and banishing spells to dispel negativity and protect against harm. The herb's soft, loving energy makes it suitable for spells promoting compassion and harmony in relationships.

Thyme

Linked to Venus and the element of water, thyme is an herb known for its hearty aroma and robust symbolism of courage, healing, and purification. Its vibrant energy has been utilized for centuries to inspire bravery and resilience. Practitioners often use thyme in spells intended to boost courage, confidence, and strength. It's also considered a powerful tool for healing spells, both emotional and physical, and is used to encourage recovery and resilience. Thyme's purifying properties make it a staple in rituals aimed at cleansing and purifying both one's physical and magical spaces—often burned in incense or used in purification baths. As a potent enhancer of psychic abilities, thyme is often employed in divination rituals, dream magic, and spells aimed at strengthening the third eye.

Rose

As an enduring symbol of love, beauty, and healing, the rose is closely tied to Venus and the element of water. It's the quintessential flower of romance, passion, and heart-centered healing, making it an integral part of love spells of all kinds—from attracting new love to deepening existing relationships. Notably, each color of rose carries additional symbolic meanings. For example, red roses are often used to symbolize romantic love, passion, and desire, while white roses symbolize purity, innocence, and spiritual love. Beyond love spells, roses also embody protective qualities and can be used in spells and rituals for protection, especially concerning matters of the heart. Additionally, rose petals can be incorporated into magical tools such as oils, waters, and incense. Rose-infused water, also known as rose water, is a popular tool for cleansing and blessing, particularly in matters related to love and beauty.

Mugwort

Connected to the moon and the element of earth, mugwort is an herb steeped in mystery and magic. Its long history of use in folk traditions and magic has established it as a potent tool for dreams, divination, and protection. Its powers are often used to enhance psychic abilities, with a particular emphasis on inducing prophetic dreams and facilitating astral projection or lucid dreaming. Drinking mugwort tea before bedtime or placing it under your pillow can enhance dream clarity and recall. The herb is also believed to provide protection during these otherworldly journeys, guarding the spirit and helping to ensure a safe return. Beyond its psychic uses, mugwort is also often used in spells for healing, purification, and protection. For instance, it can be added to smudge bundles or incense blends to cleanse and protect your space.

Cinnamon

This spicy, aromatic herb is associated with the Sun and the element of fire, representing spirituality, success, and healing. Known for its warm, invigorating properties, cinnamon is commonly used in spells to attract love and prosperity. Its association with the sun makes it a powerful tool for success and abundance, often used in money spells or job-seeking rituals. Cinnamon's ability to enhance psychic abilities makes it a favorite for divination tools, sachets, and spell jars. By fostering spiritual growth, cinnamon can help one tap into their higher self, making it a beneficial addition to meditation or rituals aimed at personal development. The herb's healing energy is also believed to boost vitality and overall wellness, making it a staple in various health and healing spells.

These are just a few examples of the many herbs used in white magic. Each herb offers its energy and symbolism, providing a multitude of ways for practitioners to enrich their magical workings. It's crucial, though, to remember that the most potent magic comes from developing a personal relationship with the herbs you work with. By growing, harvesting, or even just meditating with these herbs, you can deepen your understanding of their energies and potential uses, enhancing your white magic

Gathering, Storing, and Using Magical Herbs

The process of gathering, storing, and using herbs in white magic is as essential as understanding their individual properties and correspondences. These practices honor the life of the plants, preserve their magical properties, and enhance your connection with them.

Gathering Herbs

Time of Day: Most herbs are best gathered in the morning after the dew has dried but before the afternoon sun has drained essential oils from the plant.

Moon Phase: Some practitioners gather herbs according to moon phases, which they believe impacts the herbs' potency. A common belief is that the full moon imbues herbs with extra power, making it an optimal time for gathering.

Asking Permission: Before you cut or pick any plant, take a moment to connect with its energy and ask for permission.

This practice fosters respect for nature and recognizes the living spirit within all things.

Sustainability: Always harvest herbs in a way that promotes their growth and respects the natural ecosystem. Take only what you need and never damage the plant or its surroundings.

Storing Herbs

Drying: Most herbs are dried before storage. They can be tied in small bundles and hung upside down in a warm, dry, and dark place. Check them periodically until they're completely dry, typically in one to three weeks depending on the herb and the climate.

Containers: Once dried, herbs should be stored in airtight containers, such as glass jars, to prevent moisture and light from degrading their potency.

Labels: Always label your herbs with their name and the date of storage. This practice helps you keep track of your herbs and their freshness.

Storage Conditions: Store herbs in a cool, dark, and dry place. Heat, light, and moisture can all degrade the herbs' magical and medicinal properties over time.

Using Magical Herbs

Spell Work: Herbs can be incorporated into spells in various ways. They can be used as offerings, inscribed on candles, added to spell jars, or burnt as incense.

Ritual Baths: Herbs can be added to ritual baths for their magical properties. Always make sure the herbs are safe for skin contact before using them in this way.

Teas, Infusions, and Tinctures: Many herbs can be ingested for their magical properties, either as a tea, an infusion, or a tincture. Always ensure that the herb is safe for consumption before using it in this way, and consult a health professional if you have any concerns.

Smudging: Herbs such as sage and rosemary can be tied into bundles and dried to create smudge sticks. These are used to cleanse a space of negative energy.

Dream Pillows and Sachets: Herbs with calming or psychic-enhancing properties can be placed in dream pillows or sachets to aid in sleep or enhance dreams.

How to Make Herbal Mixtures for Spells

Creating herbal mixtures for spells is a practice that allows practitioners to harness the inherent magical properties of various herbs to accomplish a desired outcome. This process is an intimate, deeply personal act of connection with the natural world and its energies. Let's delve into the process:

Purpose Identification

The first step is to clarify the purpose of your spell. This will guide the choice of herbs to include in your mixture. Are you looking to foster love, prosperity, protection, healing, or spiritual growth? Once you've identified your intention, you can select herbs that correspond with these energies.

Herb Selection

Each herb carries a unique energetic signature and symbolism, as we've seen in the previous chapter. For example, rosemary symbolizes purification and protection, lavender is associated with peace and love, while cinnamon is connected to spirituality and success.

Choose herbs that align with your intention. It is perfectly fine to rely on your intuition for this step; what herbs feel right for your purpose? You can use a single herb or a combination, depending on your needs and the complexity of your spell.

Preparing the Herbs

Once you have your herbs selected, you will need to prepare them. If you're using fresh herbs, this might involve drying them first. If you're using dried herbs, you might want to crush or grind them into smaller pieces. A mortar and pestle is a traditional tool for this, but you can also use a herb grinder or a knife.

The act of preparing the herbs is itself part of the spell. As you work, visualize your intention, imbuing the herbs with your energy and purpose. Some practitioners like to chant, pray, or meditate during this process to enhance the connection.

Mixing the Herbs

With your herbs prepared, it's time to mix them. This can be as simple as combining them in a bowl and stirring them with your hands or a special spoon. As you mix, continue focusing on your intention. Picture the energies of the herbs intertwining, becoming more than the sum of their parts.

It's common to add a verbal component here as well, speaking your intention aloud or reciting a special incantation or affirmation. This further aligns your energies with those of the herbs.

Storing the Mixture

Once your herbal mixture is complete, it should be stored properly until it's needed. An airtight jar is ideal for this. Some practitioners prefer to use jars of certain colors, such as dark blue or amber, to block out light and preserve the herbs' energies.

Using the Mixture

Herbal mixtures can be used in a variety of ways. You might burn them as incense, carry them in a sachet, scatter them in a circle for a spell, or incorporate them into a ritual bath. Always remember to give thanks for the herbs and their energies as you use your mixture, recognizing the role they play in your magic.

Chapter Six: Moon Magic

The moon has commanded human awe and veneration since the dawn of time. Its radiant presence in the nocturnal sky has kindled an abundance of myths, doctrines, and rituals. In the domain of white magic, the moon assumes a pivotal role due to its profound sway over the earth, its cyclical nature, and the energy it emanates.

The moon is tied to the domain of emotions, intuition, and the subconscious. It's viewed as a feminine symbol, embodying qualities such as receptivity, nurture, and transformation. The lunar phases, namely new moon, waxing moon, full moon, and waning moon, each hold specific energies that can be harnessed in white magic.

New Moon: The Beginning

The New Moon phase signifies the start of the lunar cycle when the moon is directly between the Earth and the Sun, rendering it invisible to the naked eye. This stage has deep symbolic significance as it embodies the concept of beginning or initiation. Much like the dawn of a new day, the New Moon provides an opportune moment to set out on new endeavors, projects, or personal pursuits. This period is considered optimal for setting intentions—planning and marking out the path for what you aspire to achieve. In various traditions and practices such as Wicca or Neo-Paganism, the New Moon holds a sacred place.

Practitioners often engage in specific spells and rituals that align with the energy of beginnings that this lunar phase exudes. Initiating personal growth and transformation are often the central themes of these practices, with a focus on self-improvement, learning new skills, or cultivating positive habits.

Waxing Moon: Growth and Attraction

Following the New Moon, the Moon enters the Waxing phase. During this period, the visible part of the moon gradually increases, appearing to grow larger each night until it reaches the stage of the Full Moon. The waxing moon symbolizes growth, attraction, and positive transformation, mirroring its increase in the night sky. This phase is believed to be a potent time to draw positive energies and desired outcomes toward oneself. Just as the moon grows in size, so too can one's intentions and desires expand and flourish. People engaging in spiritual practices might perform specific rituals or spells under the waxing moon aimed at attraction or increase. This could be to draw love into one's life, attract prosperity or financial growth, or achieve success in a particular endeavor. The increasing illumination of the waxing moon serves as a powerful symbol of potential turning into reality, the manifestation of desires, and the unfolding of positive changes. It's a phase that resonates with abundance, progress, and growth, hence making it the perfect time to focus on and nurture one's aspirations.

Full Moon: Culmination and Realization

The Full Moon phase is the midpoint of the lunar cycle, a time when the moon is fully illuminated and appears as a perfect circle in the night sky. Symbolically, this phase represents the pinnacle of energy, clarity, and the fulfillment of intentions. It marks the culmination of efforts started during the New Moon and the fruition of desires nurtured throughout the waxing phase. The Full Moon is often associated with a heightened sense of power and psychic sensitivity. Spells and rituals performed under this phase tend to be celebratory, acknowledging the maturation of intentions set earlier in the lunar cycle, or they can be designed to leverage the potent energy for more powerful spellwork. Healing rituals, charging of magical tools, and spells aimed at amplifying energies or realizing goals are particularly associated with this period. The Full Moon is a powerful symbol of wholeness, completion, and the rewarding realization of goals or aspirations.

Waning Moon: Release and Letting Go

After the peak of the Full Moon, the lunar cycle enters the Waning phase. In this stage, the visible part of the moon decreases night by night, mirroring the concept of decline and letting go. This period invites introspection and the release of what no longer serves one's highest good. It symbolizes a time for banishing negative habits, for forgiving past grievances, and for consciously ending relationships, practices, or things that might be hindering personal growth. Spells and rituals performed during the waning moon often focus on release, cleansing, and purification. This can range from banishing negative energies or harmful habits, to facilitating forgiveness and emotional healing. The Waning Moon phase embodies the wisdom in understanding that letting go is an integral part of growth and renewal.

Dark Moon: Reflection and Rest

The Dark Moon, alternatively referred to as the Balsamic Moon, signifies the conclusion of the lunar cycle, right before the commencement of a new lunar phase. In this stage, the moon is nearly entirely hidden from Earth's view, resulting in a blackened sky. This interval is typified by introspection, repose, and preparation for the imminent cycle. It offers a sacred pause, a moment to reflect on the past cycle, to rest and heal, and to prepare for new beginnings. It's a powerful period for deep, transformative inner work, such as shadow work, which involves addressing and healing the hidden aspects of oneself. Rather than active spellwork, this time is best used for meditation, rest, and reflection, as one prepares mentally and spiritually for the cycle of growth and manifestation that will begin anew with the New Moon. The Dark Moon signifies a moment of closure, reflection, and the promise of regeneration.

Lunar Spell Timing

One of the key principles of white magic is the alignment of personal intention with the natural rhythms of the cosmos. In this regard, the moon and its phases hold profound significance. By timing spells and rituals according to the lunar cycle, the practitioner can attune to the ebb and flow of lunar energy, enhancing the effectiveness and resonance of their magical workings.

Here, we will delve deeper into the concept of lunar spell timing:

New Moon Spells

The New Moon, representing the start of the lunar cycle, provides a potent window for the casting of spells that are aligned with new beginnings and fresh ventures. During this phase, the moon is not visible in the sky, creating a symbolic darkness that anticipates rebirth and renewal. This is an opportune moment for crafting and casting spells that initiate new projects, relationships, or life changes. The energy during the New Moon phase is especially receptive to intentions related to starting afresh. For example, if you are embarking on a new career path, initiating a new relationship, or launching a personal project, a spell crafted and performed during the New Moon can help in setting the energy and intention for success. The New Moon phase also supports spells for visioning and planning. Spells focused on setting clear goals, visualizing success, or manifesting dreams into reality can be particularly powerful during this period.

Waxing Moon Spells

The Waxing Moon phase, during which the moon visibly increases in size from a slim crescent to a half-moon, symbolizes a period of growth, construction, and attraction. The growing moon reflects increasing energy and momentum, making it an ideal time for spells that are meant to draw desired outcomes toward you. Spells performed during the waxing moon can be crafted to attract a variety of positive energies or outcomes. Whether you're working towards attracting love, financial abundance, professional success, or healing energy, the waxing moon is an opportune time for such spellwork. Moreover, the waxing phase supports spells aimed at self-improvement and growth. For instance, if you wish to enhance certain skills, foster positive personal traits, or improve your health and vitality, performing a spell during the waxing moon phase can enhance these intentions and help you manifest your desires more effectively.

Full Moon Spells

The Full Moon embodies the apex of the lunar cycle when lunar energy is at its crest. In this phase, the moon is fully lit, making it an exceptionally potent period for casting spells, especially those necessitating a substantial amount of energy or those targeting considerable changes. Full Moon magic is versatile and can be tailored to various purposes, such as protection spells, divination, or manifestation of long-term goals. The energy of the Full Moon can amplify the potency of your magical workings, making it an ideal time to conduct spells of great importance. Furthermore, the Full Moon's energy can be harnessed for charging magical tools like crystals, tarot cards, or amulets. By exposing these items to the light of the Full Moon, they can absorb its potent energy, enhancing their effectiveness in future magical workings.

Waning Moon Spells

The Waning Moon phase, during which the moon decreases in size from a half-moon to a sliver before disappearing completely, symbolizes a period of decline, release, and letting go. This phase provides an opportune time for spells that aim to diminish or eliminate aspects of your life. If your intent is to release negative emotions, break harmful habits, or sever toxic relationships, casting your spells during the waning moon can lend added force to your intentions. Spells for banishment, release, and purification are particularly potent during this period, allowing for a purging of what no longer serves you and creating space for positive growth and change.

Dark Moon Spells

This phase is characterized by rest, introspection, and preparation for the next cycle. Instead of active spell work, the Dark Moon invites us to engage in introspective practices, focusing on self-reflection, meditation, and journaling. This period is perfect for releasing old patterns and outdated narratives, clearing the slate for new intentions and possibilities in the coming cycle. Spells or rituals during the Dark Moon may focus on deep transformative work, uncovering hidden aspects of oneself, and healing shadow parts. This phase provides a tranquil space for the preparation and readiness required for the new beginnings heralded by the upcoming New Moon.

Making Moon Water

Moon water is simply water that has been charged under the energy of the moon. While it can be made during any phase, it's often prepared under the full moon to capture the peak of lunar energy. The process is simple:

- Start with a clean, preferably glass container. Fill it with purified or natural spring water.

- Set your intention. This might be for healing, purification, abundance, or any other purpose that aligns with your needs and the current moon phase.

- Place the water under the moonlight. Leave it there overnight, allowing the lunar energy to infuse the water.

- Retrieve it before the sun rises to maintain the lunar purity of the water.

- Store it in a cool, dark place until it's needed.

Moon water can be used in a variety of ways: as an ingredient in spellwork, for cleansing ritual tools, or simply for drinking to absorb the moon's energy.

Charging Crystals

In the same way that the moon's energy can imbue water with vitality and purify it, it can also cleanse and energize crystals. This practice is especially powerful during the Full Moon phase when the lunar energy is at its zenith. To charge your crystals, it's necessary to subject them to moonlight. This can be accomplished by positioning them on a windowsill, an outdoor area, or any place where they can be directly bathed in moonlight. Leaving them overnight allows the crystals to absorb the moon's energy fully. By the morning, the crystals are charged, cleansed, and ready for use.

Once charged, these crystals can serve multiple purposes. They can amplify your intentions, aiding in manifestation work, spellcasting, or goal-setting. They can be used in meditation to enhance focus, or even in healing practices for their energetic properties. Additionally, charged crystals can function as protective talismans, warding off negative energies.

Different crystals correspond to different intentions and energies. For example, rose quartz is often used for love spells or heart healing, while amethyst is known for its calming and intuitive properties. Therefore, when charging crystals, it's important to select them according to your needs, intentions, and the specific phase of the moon. This can create a synergy between the lunar energy, the inherent properties of the crystal, and your personal intention, making your spellwork, meditation, or healing work even more effective.

Moonlight Meditations

Meditating under the moonlight is a profound way to connect with the lunar energy and your own inner wisdom. This practice can be especially potent during the Full Moon when the lunar energy is at its strongest, but meditating during other phases can also help you synchronize with the specific energy of that particular phase. For instance, meditating during the New Moon can support the setting of new intentions, while a meditation during the Waning Moon might focus more on letting go.

Moonlight meditations can be guided, following a predetermined path or theme, or they can be free-form, allowing you to intuitively explore your inner landscape under the moon's light. Regardless of the format, the focus should be on the moon, your connection to its energy, and your personal intentions or goals. Visualizing the moonlight filling your body can facilitate a deeper connection to lunar energy, while also enhancing the clarity of your intentions. By consciously aligning yourself with the moon's phases and energies, you can harness its power to bring about greater self-awareness, emotional healing, and spiritual growth.

Lunar Divination

The phases of the moon offer significant insights in various divination practices such as tarot reading, rune casting, or even scrying. Each phase of the moon carries its own energy and symbolism, providing an additional layer of context for the interpretations of your readings. For instance, a divination conducted during the New Moon may speak more to beginnings, potential, and latent opportunities, while one performed under the Full Moon may suggest culmination, fulfillment, or realization. Similarly, the Waning Moon might be interpreted as a time of release, while the Waxing Moon suggests growth and attraction.

Some practitioners also use the moon itself as a divination tool, a practice known as Selenomancy. They may observe the moon's appearance, phase, or even its halo and interpret the patterns or peculiarities as signs and omens. Such practices provide a direct interaction with lunar energy and can offer unique insights aligning with the natural rhythm of the lunar cycle.

Moon Bathing

Moon bathing, a practice similar to sunbathing, involves soaking up the energy of the moonlight. It can be as simple as sitting or lying under the moon's glow, consciously absorbing its energy. Moon bathing can serve as a form of meditation, a time for quiet contemplation, or a cleansing ritual to recharge your personal energy.

This ritual is especially powerful during the Full Moon phase, when lunar energy is at its zenith. As you luxuriate in the moon's glow, envision its energy swathing and suffusing your body, purging you of any adverse influences and replenishing you with its radiant life force. Moon bathing can promote tranquility, foster a deep sense of connection with nature, and revitalize your personal energy. By tuning into the moon's energy in such a direct, physical way, you allow its rhythmic cycle to harmonize with your own energy, promoting balance and wellbeing.

Chapter Seven: Spellcasting Basics

In the realm of white magic, intent is the heart of any spell. It is the force that gives life to your magic, that shapes and directs your energy towards the goal you seek to achieve. Crafting clear, focused intent is thus a foundational skill in any magical practice, serving as the seed from which your spells grow and flourish.

Let's explore how you can craft a powerful and effective intent:

Identify Your True Desire

Identifying your true desire is the initial and most crucial step in crafting your intention. It requires a deep dive into self-exploration and honest reflection. On the surface, it might seem that your desires are straightforward. However, it is often the case that our immediate wants are actually symptoms or expressions of deeper, more profound needs. For instance, desiring a new job might actually be a manifestation of a deeper need for a sense of purpose, satisfaction, or fulfillment in your work. To truly understand your desires, dedicate time for introspection, perhaps through meditation or journaling. Uncover the real essence of your desire, the fundamental need that drives it. The more genuine and aligned your intention is with your core needs, the more potent your magic becomes, as it is imbued with the authenticity of your true self.

Be Specific

After discerning your true longing, the ensuing step is to delineate it as accurately as you can. The preciseness of your intention is crucial as it gives a distinct target for your energy to aim at. If your desire is to find a new job, for instance, delve into the particulars of this goal. What kind of job are you seeking? What responsibilities do you want to have? What work environment suits you best? What qualities are you looking for in your colleagues and supervisors? By visualizing the minute details of your goal, you create a vivid and tangible picture, thereby facilitating its manifestation into reality.

Frame It Positively

The way you articulate your intention significantly influences the outcomes of your magic. Consequently, it's vital to phrase your intention positively. Instead of centering on what you hope to expunge or evade in your life, focus on what you aspire to magnetize or foster. For example, if your objective is to bolster your health, rather than setting an intention to "avoid illness," strive for "attaining a state of holistic health and vigor." This positive phrasing attracts the desired outcomes towards you, in contrast to repelling unwanted circumstances. A positive frame not only enhances your vibrational frequency, making attraction more likely, but it also encourages a positive mindset, which can have wide-ranging benefits in your life.

Connect It to Your Emotions

Intent becomes more powerful when it's tied to the emotional experience that achieving the goal will bring. This emotional engagement helps to increase the vibrational energy that you're sending out into the universe. When you're crafting your intention, consider the emotions that achieving this goal would stir within you. Would it be joy, satisfaction, tranquility, or perhaps a sense of love? Engage with these emotions as you construct and hold your intention. This not only enhances the potency of your intent, but also makes the entire magical process more satisfying and meaningful. Plus, your emotional connection to your goal will serve as motivation and will keep you focused and committed throughout your journey.

State It In Present Tense

The way you phrase your intention is also vital in shaping its effectiveness. When articulating your intent, use the present tense as if your goal is a current reality. This technique affirms your faith in your intention's potential and aligns your energetic frequency with that of your desired manifestation. For instance, instead of stating, "I will have a fulfilling job," you would say, "I am thriving in my fulfilling and satisfying job." This approach essentially tells the universe that you are ready to receive your manifestation now, and it helps to attract that reality into your life.

Make It Harm None

In accordance with the ethics of white magic, it's paramount that your intention harms no one. This means respecting the free will of others and avoiding intentions that seek to manipulate or control others for your benefit. As a practitioner of white magic, your goal should always be for the highest good of all concerned. Ensuring that your intention is harm-free not only adheres to the ethical principles of white magic, but it also ensures that the energy you are projecting into the world is positive and constructive. Remember, the energy you send out is the energy you attract back, so fostering benevolent intentions is not only ethically sound, but it's also beneficial for your personal spiritual journey.

Creating and Closing a Magic Circle

A magic circle is a sacred space where practitioners of white magic conduct their rituals, spells, and meditations. It serves as a boundary between the physical and spiritual worlds, a protective barrier shielding you from outside influences, and a container for the energy you raise during your work. Here's how you can create and close a magic circle:

Creating a Magic Circle

Choose Your Space: A circle can be cast indoors or outdoors, but the location should be somewhere you feel comfortable and safe. It should be large enough for you to move around in freely, and clean and tidy to facilitate clear energy flow.

Gather Your Tools: While some practitioners use specific tools such as a ritual sword or wand to cast their circles, this is not necessary. Your finger, a stick, or even just your mind and intentions can serve just as effectively.

Purify the Space: Before you begin, cleanse the space physically and energetically. You might physically clean the area, then smudge it with sage, sweep it with a besom, or sprinkle it with saltwater. This purifies the space and prepares it for your magic.

Set Your Intention: Decide on the purpose of the circle. Is it for a ritual, a spell, meditation, or something else? Your intention will help shape the energy of the circle.

Cast the Circle: Stand in the center of your space, facing east. Extend your casting tool or your hand towards the edge of the circle. Imagine a beam of light extending from your tool or hand, and use it to draw a circle around you. As you do, visualize the circle as a sphere of light enveloping you, extending both above and below.

Call in the Elements: Once your circle is cast, you might choose to call in the elements. Start in the east (air), then turn to the south (fire), west (water), and finally north (earth). As you face each direction, invite the element to lend its energy to your circle.

Invoke Higher Powers: Depending on your practice, you might invoke deities, ancestors, spirit guides, or universal energy. Ask them to join you in your circle and aid in your work.

Your circle is now cast, and you can proceed with your magic. Remember, what happens in the circle should be in line with your intentions.

Closing a Magic Circle

Thank Higher Powers: If you invoked any higher powers, thank them for their assistance and bid them farewell.

Release the Elements: Turn to each cardinal point again, thank the element associated with that direction, and politely ask it to depart. Start with the north (earth), west (water), south (fire), and finally east (air).

Close the Circle: Facing east again, raise your casting tool or hand. Visualize the circle's energy being drawn back into the tool or your body. Move in the opposite direction to which you cast the circle, usually counterclockwise, seeing the circle dissolve as you go.

Ground Your Energy: After the circle is closed, take a moment to ground. This might involve eating something, visualizing excess energy returning to the earth, or simply sitting quietly for a moment.

Steps of a Successful Spellcast

Spellcasting is an integral part of white magic, serving as a practical application of the energy manipulation skills and ethical considerations central to this path. A successful spellcast requires careful planning, clarity of intent, and a respectful approach towards the forces you're working with. Below are the key steps for a successful spellcast:

1. Plan Your Spell

Planning your spell is an essential step in the magical process. This necessitates thoughtful contemplation of the optimal moment to cast the spell, taking into consideration various factors like celestial happenings, lunar phases, and the specific day within the week. Each of these components harbors unique energies that can amplify the efficacy of your spell. For instance, a love spell might be most effective when cast on a Friday, the day of the week associated with Venus, the planet of love.

2. Create Sacred Space

Prior to beginning your spell, it's crucial to create a sacred space, often accomplished by casting a magical circle. This circle serves as a boundary, separating the physical world from the spiritual realm, and provides a protective barrier against external influences. When casting your circle, set a clear intention for this space to be filled with love, light, and positive energy. You might do this through visualization, imagining a bright light surrounding you, or through ritual, physically marking out the circle with stones, crystals, or other symbolic objects.

3. Invoke the Elements or Deities

Depending on your personal beliefs and the nature of your spell, the next step might involve invoking the elements (Earth, Air, Fire, and Water), deities, spirit guides, ancestors, or any other higher powers that resonate with you. This involves inviting these energies or entities into your sacred space, asking for their assistance in your spellcasting. This invocation can be a formal ritual, a simple spoken request, or a silent, heartfelt intention. Remember to approach this process with respect and gratitude, acknowledging the power and wisdom these entities bring to your work.

4. Raise Energy

To cast your spell, you'll need to raise energy. This can be done in a variety of ways depending on what feels right for you. Some people raise energy through visualization, imagining a light or force within them growing brighter and stronger with each breath. Others might use chanting, repeating a word or phrase that aligns with their intent, or physical movement like dancing. Regardless of the method you choose, the goal is to generate and channel energy towards your intent. This raised energy acts as a driving force, propelling your intent into the universe and aiding in its manifestation.

5. Direct the Energy

Once you've raised a substantial amount of energy during your spellcasting process, the following step is to channel it towards your objective. Concentrate on your intent, visualizing it as vividly as you possibly can. Picture your desired outcome in your mind, and feel it in your heart. Now, imagine the energy you've raised flowing into this envisioned scenario, imbuing it with life and power. Some practitioners may choose to direct this energy using tools such as a wand or athame, while others simply use their hands or even just their intention.

6. Ground Your Energy

After casting your spell, grounding your energy is a critical step. This process involves releasing any surplus energy you've raised during your spell, letting it flow into the earth. Envision the energy moving down through your body, out through your feet, and into the ground. Grounding not only prevents potential energy overload or imbalance, which could lead to feeling jittery, scattered, or exhausted, but it also helps to bring your spellwork into the physical realm, aiding in its manifestation.

7. Close Your Circle

With the spell now complete and your energy grounded, the next phase is to close your circle. This involves thanking any entities you have invoked during your ritual. Show gratitude for their assistance, bid them farewell, and respectfully request their departure. As you close your circle, visualize the energy of the circle dispersing and dissipating, yet leaving the clear, potent energy of your spell remaining. Some traditions also involve physically closing the circle, walking in the opposite direction to which it was cast and visualizing it closing behind them.

8. Allow the Spell to Manifest

The concluding step in the spellcasting process is to have faith in the spell you've cast and to allow the universe time and space to let it manifest. This might require patience, as spells don't always manifest immediately or in the ways we expect. Know that your intentions have been projected into the universe and that the wheels are in motion. In the meantime, continue to hold your intent in your mind, nurturing it with positive thoughts and actions, and remain open to signs and opportunities that your spell is manifesting.

The Book of Shadows

A Book of Shadows is an essential tool for any practitioner of white magic. Often seen as a magical diary, it's a personal record of your magical journey, your spellwork, experiences, insights, and growth as a practitioner. Maintaining a Book of Shadows can not only aid in reflection and progression but also create a valuable resource to look back on in your practice. Let's dive deeper into the significance and structure of this sacred book.

Purpose of a Book of Shadows

Record Keeping: The Book of Shadows is your private journal for keeping track of your magical workings. It includes records of spells, rituals, the results of those activities, notes about different magical tools and materials you used, and your thoughts and feelings about your practice. This process helps create a timeline of your development and the evolution of your understanding of white magic.

Personal Reflection: Your BoS is a place to reflect on your spiritual and magical journey. By writing about your experiences, you may notice patterns or insights that you might not have recognized otherwise. These entries can serve as valuable points of introspection and spiritual growth.

Learning Resource: Over time, your Book of Shadows becomes a compendium of your acquired knowledge. It contains all your trials, errors, and successes, providing you a unique learning resource that caters specifically to your personal practice.

Creating Your Book of Shadows

Choose Your Book: Your Book of Shadows can be as simple or as elaborate as you wish. It could be a beautifully bound leather journal, a simple notebook, or even a digital document. The key is that it should feel personal and meaningful to you.

Dedicate Your Book: Before you begin writing in your Book of Shadows, you might choose to perform a small dedication ritual. This could involve cleansing the book with sage or incense, blessing it in the light of the moon, or saying a small prayer or affirmation of intent. This process serves to cleanse it of any pre-existing energies and align it with your personal energies.

What to Include in Your Book of Shadows

Here are some ideas of what you might include in your BoS:

Spells and Rituals: Document any spells or rituals you perform, including the date, purpose, materials used, procedure followed, and results observed.

Magical Tools: Keep a record of the magical tools you acquire, how you consecrate them, and what you use them for.

Divination Readings: If you use divination techniques like tarot, runes, or pendulums, you might record significant readings and your interpretations.

Dreams and Visions: Record any significant dreams, meditations, or visions. These could hold important messages or insights.

Observations and Reflections: Write about your observations and reflections on your magical practice, spiritual growth, and experiences with the divine.

Information and Research: Your BoS can be a repository of knowledge about different aspects of white magic such as crystals, herbs, moon phases, sabbats, and more.

Personal Symbols and Sigils: Document any personal symbols or sigils you create and the meanings behind them.

A Book of Shadows is a living document, one that evolves and grows with you on your magical journey. It is a mirror to your soul's journey in the magical realm, and hence, is one of the most personal and sacred tools in white magic.

Chapter Eight: Common White Magic Spells

White magic spells are used for positive change and are based on an intention that is in alignment with the Wiccan Rede, "An it harm none, do what ye will." This central tenet ensures that white magic spells are wielded for benevolent, uplifting, and healing purposes. As a practitioner, you're granted access to a broad array of spells crafted for a myriad of purposes. Here are some prevalent white magic spells that may prove useful in your practice:

Protection

A protection spell serves as one of the most fundamental and essential components of white magic. This sort of spell is employed to forge a protective shield around you or a cherished one, acting as a safeguard against negative energies or harm. Protection spells can be adapted to cater to specific requirements, such as securing your home, defending against harmful energies, or fortifying your aura.

Healing

Healing spells are utilized to foster physical, emotional, or spiritual restoration. It's crucial to understand that while healing spells can assist in the recovery process, they are not an alternative to medical treatment. Instead, they work harmoniously with conventional medicine, accelerating the healing journey and amplifying overall wellness.

Prosperity

Prosperity spells are employed to draw abundance and wealth. These spells can be fine-tuned to various facets of prosperity, such as attracting monetary wealth, securing a job, or garnering success in business pursuits. Remember, the goal is not to harm or deprive others, but to magnetize abundance into your own life.

Love

In the context of white magic, love spells aren't about asserting control or manipulating the emotions of others. Rather, these spells concentrate on attracting love, cultivating self-love, healing from emotional wounds, or fortifying existing relationships. These spells aim to open your heart and align you with the universal energy of love.

Peace and Harmony

These spells are harnessed to cultivate peace and harmony, whether within your own self, your household, or a particular situation. They can be used to disperse negative energies, minimize conflicts, and foster understanding and communication.

Purification

Purification spells are employed to cleanse negative energies and purify a space, object, or individual. These spells prove particularly useful when transitioning into a new home, post a dispute, or during periods of stress or transition.

Divination

Divination spells are utilized to augment your intuitive faculties and enhance the precision of your divination practices, such as tarot reading or scrying. They can aid you in establishing a connection with your higher self, spirit guides, or the universal consciousness, enabling you to procure deeper insights and guidance.

Personal Growth

These spells are oriented towards personal evolution and spiritual growth. They can assist you in attaining clarity, overcoming hurdles, fostering confidence, or releasing unhealthy habits or relationships.

Protection and Cleansing Spells

As practitioners of white magic, we recognize the importance of maintaining clear, positive energies around us and protecting ourselves from any harmful influences. This often calls for the regular use of protection and cleansing spells. These spells can help us safeguard our personal energy, cleanse our surroundings, and strengthen our overall spiritual wellbeing. Here are a few essential protection and cleansing spells that can be beneficial in your practice.

Personal Energy Shield Spell

This spell is designed to create an energetic shield around you, providing protection from negative energies or psychic attacks.

Materials needed: Your own focused intention and visualization.

Steps:

1. Sit in a quiet space where you won't be disturbed. Take a few deep breaths, grounding and centering yourself.

2. Visualize a bright, white light emanating from your heart center, expanding outward to form a shield around your entire body.

3. As you visualize this shield, affirm your intention, saying something like, "I am safe and protected in this light. No negative energies can penetrate this shield."

4. Sit with this visualization for as long as feels necessary, and then gently bring your focus back to your physical surroundings.

Home Protection Spell

This spell is used to protect your living space from any negative or harmful energies.

Materials needed: Salt, water, and your focused intention.

Steps:

1. Mix a tablespoon of salt into a bowl of water. Salt is known for its cleansing and protective properties.

2. Dip your fingers into the water and mark your doors and windows with a pentacle, an ancient symbol of protection.

3. As you do this, state your intention, saying something like, "With this symbol, I protect this home and all who dwell within. Only love and light may enter."

Cleansing Spell for Objects

Sometimes, objects can harbor residual energies from past owners or situations. This simple spell can cleanse these objects.

Materials needed: Sage bundle or incense, the object to be cleansed.

Steps:

1. Light the sage or incense. Hold the object in the smoke, rotating it to ensure the smoke reaches all sides.

2. As you do this, visualize any negative energies being lifted and carried away by the smoke. State your intention, saying something like, "With this smoke, I cleanse this object of all negative energies."

Aura Cleansing Spell

Our auras can pick up and hold onto unwanted energies. This spell can cleanse your aura.

Materials needed: A bowl of salt water, white candle.

Steps:

1. Light the candle, representing the cleansing fire. Stand before the candle.

2. Dip your hands into the bowl of salt water, then shake off the excess.

3. Starting at your head and moving downward, sweep your hands through your aura, about 6-12 inches away from your body, visualizing any negative energy being drawn out and sent into the earth.

4. Repeat your intention, saying something like, "With this water, I cleanse my aura, letting go of all that no longer serves me."

The key to effective spellcasting is a strong, focused intention. Believing in the work you are doing and trusting in the process are crucial. Additionally, regularly practicing these spells can not only maintain your personal and environmental energetic hygiene but also deepen your relationship with your magic, leading to even more powerful results.

Love and Friendship Spells

White magic places a great emphasis on love, compassion, and connection, values that resonate deeply within us as humans. Love and friendship spells in white magic are designed to invite more love into your life, improve existing relationships, and help form new, genuine connections. However, it's essential to remember that these spells must not infringe on anyone's free will or be used with the intent to manipulate others. With respect and a sincere heart, let's explore some love and friendship spells:

Love Attraction Spell

This spell is designed to open your heart and raise your vibrational frequency to attract love into your life.

Materials needed: Rose quartz, a pink candle, and your focused intention.

Steps:

1. Light the pink candle, signifying love and emotional healing.

2. Hold the rose quartz in your hand, feeling its energy. This stone is associated with unconditional love and positivity.

3. Close your eyes and visualize the kind of love you want to attract. Feel the feelings associated with being in such a relationship.

4. As you hold the rose quartz, say your intention aloud, such as, "I open my heart to give and receive love. I attract a deep, meaningful, and respectful love relationship into my life."

5. Let the candle burn down naturally while you continue to visualize your intention.

Friendship Spell

This spell can help draw new friends and strengthen existing friendships.

Materials needed: An orange candle (symbolizing attraction and friendship), a piece of paper, a pen, and your focused intention.

Steps:

1. Light the orange candle, dedicating it to friendship.

2. On the piece of paper, write down the qualities you seek in a friend or those you wish to strengthen in existing friendships.

3. As you write, visualize yourself enjoying the company of your friends, experiencing laughter, joy, support, and shared moments.

4. Fold the paper and hold it in your hands, saying something like, "I attract friendships that are mutually supportive, joyful, and authentic. May my friendships be strengthened and my circle be widened."

5. Safely burn the paper in the flame of the candle, releasing your intention to the universe.

Self-Love Spell

Before we can truly love others, we must first love ourselves. This spell is for enhancing self-love and acceptance.

Materials needed: A mirror, a pink candle, rose oil (optional), and your focused intention.

Steps:

1. Kindle the pink candle. If at hand, dab it with a few droplets of rose oil, symbolizing love.

2. Stand in front of a mirror and stare into your own eyes.

3. Chant self-love affirmations into your reflection, such as, "I deserve to be loved," "I accept myself unconditionally," and "I am grateful for who I am."

4. As you say these affirmations, try to genuinely feel the love for yourself. You may also visualize yourself surrounded by a loving, pink light.

5. End with a statement of intention, such as, "Each day, I grow in love for myself, nurturing my spirit and honoring my journey."

Love and friendship spells can be powerful tools for manifesting relationships that enrich our lives. Embrace the magic within you, and let it guide you toward the love and friendship you deserve.

Prosperity Spells

In the practice of white magic, abundance is not limited to financial prosperity. It extends to a richness of experiences, relationships, health, and overall well-being. That said, financial prosperity often plays a crucial role in facilitating our dreams and ambitions. The key to abundance and prosperity spells is the attitude of gratitude—being thankful for what we have to attract more of the same. Here are a few spells focused on attracting abundance and prosperity.

Money Attraction Spell

This spell helps draw financial abundance into your life.

Materials needed: A green candle (symbolizing prosperity), a coin, and your focused intention.

Steps:

1. Light the green candle and focus on its flame.

2. Hold the coin in your hand and visualize the abundance you wish to attract, whether it's more money, a better job, or financial stability. Feel the feelings associated with having this abundance.

3. State your intention, saying something like, "I attract wealth and prosperity. Money flows to me easily and continuously."

4. Place the coin somewhere you'll see it regularly as a reminder of your intention.

Abundance Jar Spell

This spell is intended to attract an abundance of blessings into your life.

Materials needed: A small jar, a piece of paper, a pen, coins, small crystals or stones, herbs like basil and cinnamon (associated with prosperity), and your focused intention.

Steps:

1. On the piece of paper, write what you wish to have more of in your life. It could be love, happiness, wealth, health, etc.

2. Fold the paper and place it in the jar.

3. Fill the jar with the coins, crystals, and herbs, visualizing each object amplifying your intention.

4. As you fill the jar, say something like, "I am open to receive an abundance of blessings. I am thankful for all the prosperity that flows into my life."

5. Seal the jar and place it somewhere you will see it regularly, allowing its presence to serve as a constant reminder of your intention.

Employment Spell

If you're seeking a new job or want to improve your career prospects, this spell can help.

Materials needed: A yellow candle (representing success and intellect), a piece of paper, a pen, and your focused intention.

Steps:

1. Light the yellow candle and focus on its flame.

2. Write down what kind of job you want or the career advancements you desire on the piece of paper.

3. Visualize yourself already having achieved these career goals, feeling the satisfaction and joy.

4. Fold the paper and hold it over the flame (be careful not to burn your fingers), saying something like, "I attract the perfect job that brings me fulfillment and prosperity."

5. Burn the paper safely in a fireproof bowl or container, releasing your intention into the universe.

If your desire for abundance and prosperity is genuine and harm none, the universe will conspire to help you. Believe in your magic, practice gratitude, and be ready to welcome the prosperity that comes your way.

Healing and Well-being Spells

The capacity to recuperate ourselves and others physically, candidly and profoundly is profoundly inserted in our being. Let's explore some healing and well-being spells:

General Healing Spell

This spell can be used to boost physical healing and recovery.

Materials needed: A blue candle (representing healing), a small piece of clear quartz (known for its healing properties), and your focused intention.

Steps:

1. Light the blue candle and focus on its flame, letting your mind become still.

2. Hold the clear quartz in your hand and visualize the person in need of healing (it could be you) as being completely healthy and vibrant.

3. Say your intention, something like, "I (or name of the person) am healthy and strong. Every cell in my body is vibrant with the energy of wellness."

4. Allow the candle to burn down naturally while you hold the image of the healed person in your mind.

Emotional Healing Spell

This spell is meant to aid in healing emotional wounds and bringing peace.

Materials needed: A pink candle (for love and emotional healing), a piece of rose quartz (for love and emotional healing), and your focused intention.

Steps:

1. Light the pink candle and hold the rose quartz in your hand.

2. Close your eyes and visualize the emotional pain being replaced with healing energy.

3. Speak your intention, such as, "I am healed. I release all emotional pain and open my heart to peace and love."

4. Allow the candle to burn out naturally, releasing your healing intention into the universe.

Stress Relief Spell

This spell is designed to help reduce stress and promote relaxation.

Materials needed: A white candle (for peace), lavender incense or essential oil (for relaxation), and your focused intention.

Steps:

1. Light the white candle and the lavender incense.

2. Sit comfortably and take a few deep breaths, inhaling the calming scent of lavender.

3. As you breathe out, visualize your stress and worries leaving your body.

4. Speak your intention, such as, "I release all stress and tension. I am calm and at peace."

5. Allow the candle and incense to burn out naturally as you continue to breathe deeply and relax.

Well-Sleep Spell

This spell can be used to encourage a good night's sleep free from nightmares.

Materials needed: A purple candle (for peace and spirituality), a piece of amethyst (known for promoting calm and good dreams), and your focused intention.

Steps:

1. Light the purple candle and hold the amethyst in your hand.

2. Visualize yourself falling asleep easily and having a peaceful, restful sleep.

3. Speak your intention, such as, "I sleep easily and peacefully. I awake refreshed and filled with positive energy."

4. Leave the amethyst by your bed and allow the candle to burn out safely.

White magic provides a path to improve our overall wellness and help us heal from various physical and emotional wounds. The power of these spells lies in your belief and the positive intention behind your actions. Remember to always pair these spells with appropriate medical advice and treatment when needed. As above, so below, as within, so without, let the healing begin.

Chapter Nine: Advanced Techniques in White Magic

As we delve further into the world of white magic, we come across advanced techniques that require a higher level of understanding, intention, and practice. These are not necessarily more complicated but demand greater dedication, time, and energy. Remember, magic should always be performed responsibly, with a clear purpose and respect for the forces you're dealing with. These practices are for those who've already found their grounding in the basic principles and ethics of white magic.

Divination Techniques

Divination, a practice that's been present in cultures worldwide, is a key component of white magic. At its heart, divination is the practice of seeking insights or answers through various ritualistic techniques. It can function as a tool for self-reflection, a source of guidance for decision-making, or simply a conduit to connect more intimately with the universe's wisdom. Below are some typical divination methods used within the sphere of white magic:

Tarot Reading

Within the scope of white magic, the Tarot is a potent divination instrument, acting as a mirror to our souls and a compass on our spiritual voyages. Its elaborate symbolism and profound wisdom can illuminate the enigmas of our lives, empowering us to comprehend our innermost selves and maneuver the world around us.

Tarot Deck: A standard Tarot deck encompasses 78 cards, bifurcated into two primary sections: The Major Arcana and the Minor Arcana. The Major Arcana, consisting of 22 cards, signifies significant life events and spiritual lessons. Each card, starting from The Fool and ending with The World, represents stages in a journey towards self-realization and spiritual enlightenment.

The Minor Arcana includes 56 cards divided into four suits - Wands, Cups, Swords, and Pentacles - each relating to a different aspect of life. Wands represent the realm of spirit and inspiration, Cups correspond to emotions and relationships, Swords indicate intellect and conflict, and Pentacles refer to material aspects and practical matters.

Tarot Reading Works: A Tarot reading begins with a question or an intention. This doesn't necessarily have to be a specific query; it can be a general request for guidance. After formulating the question, the practitioner shuffles the Tarot deck, focusing on the question or intention while doing so.

Next comes laying out the cards in a specific pattern, known as a spread. The spread can be as simple as a single-card draw or as complex as the ten-card Celtic Cross spread. Each position in the spread has a unique significance that contributes to the overall interpretation.

Reading the cards involves interpreting the symbolism of each card and its position within the spread, and intuitively piecing together the story they tell. It's essential to note that the Tarot does not predict a fixed or inevitable future. Instead, it presents potential outcomes based on current energies and offers insights into the forces influencing a situation.

Interpreting Tarot Cards: Each Tarot card holds a spectrum of meanings, influenced by its imagery, symbolism, numerology, and elemental associations. The context of the reading and the intuition of the reader also play a crucial role in the interpretation. The same card can convey different messages in different readings.

A reversed Tarot card, which appears upside down in a reading, often indicates an internal or blocked energy relating to the card's meaning or a need to pay extra attention to that card's aspect.

Pendulum Dowsing

In the world of white magic, pendulum dowsing serves as a revered tool for divination and decision-making. Harnessing the subtle energy fields around us, it offers insightful guidance and deepens our connection with our intuition. The pendulum, fundamentally, acts as an extension of our inner beings and the unseen energetic dimensions that sculpt our existence.

In its simplest form, a pendulum is a symmetrical object, carrying weight, suspended from a stationary point. While pendulums can be crafted from a variety of materials, those employed in dowsing are typically fashioned from metal or crystal. The pendulum's structure allows it to swing in various directions, with the direction of the swing interpreted as meaningful responses to questions or statements.

How Pendulum Dowsing Work: The fundamental concept behind pendulum dowsing is that our subconscious minds are connected to the universal consciousness, and therefore, have access to all knowledge. When we ask a question of the pendulum, we are, in fact, tapping into this universal consciousness, our higher selves, or our spirit guides, depending on your belief system.

Before beginning a pendulum dowsing session, you must establish a clear understanding of what each movement of the pendulum signifies. For many, a swing back and forth represents 'yes,' a side-to-side motion signifies 'no,' and a circular motion or stillness can indicate 'maybe' or 'question unclear.'

Using the Pendulum: When you begin to dowse, hold the pendulum in a steady hand, and ask it a simple yes/no question to which you already know the answer. This helps to establish trust in the pendulum's movements and creates a clear communication channel. Once you're confident in your pendulum's responses, you can proceed to ask it more complex or unknown questions.

Always approach dowsing with an open and clear mind. Your intent and concentration should be geared towards uncovering the truth and receiving guidance, not aiming for a specific outcome.

Applications of Pendulum Dowsing: Pendulum dowsing can be employed in a multitude of contexts. Some practitioners utilize it to procure answers to personal queries or to aid in decision-making. Others harness it to discern energy fields and balances, frequently in the sphere of healing endeavors. It can serve as an invaluable instrument for meditation and personal development, assisting in clarifying emotions, thoughts, and subconscious longings.

Scrying

In the realm of white magic, scrying is a time-honored method of divination. It involves gazing into a reflective or translucent surface to perceive visions or insights. As an introspective and intuitive practice, scrying enables us to tap into our subconscious mind and the wider web of collective consciousness, providing a window into hidden truths and potential futures.

Scrying derives from the Old English word 'descry,' which means 'to reveal.' This form of divination has a rich history, tracing back centuries, appearing in an array of cultures throughout time. Notably, the ancient Egyptians, Greeks, and Celts were known to employ scrying as a method to perceive beyond the physical realm.

Scrying can encompass a broad variety of surfaces for contemplation. Popular implements include mirrors (particularly black mirrors), crystal balls, bowls filled with water, fire, and even the wavering glow of a candle flame. The objective is not to concentrate on the physical reflection, but to gaze through it, permitting the mind's eye to unlock and reveal visions and insights.

Scrying isn't about straining or 'trying hard' to perceive something. Rather, it's about relaxation, letting go, and allowing images to present themselves to you. To begin, choose a quiet and comfortable space where you can focus. You might like to create a sacred space, perhaps lighting a candle or invoking a circle of protection before you begin.

Hold your gaze softly on your chosen surface and allow your eyes to lose focus. As you gaze, you might start to see shapes, colors, symbols, or even full images. These aren't typically sharp, clear visions, but more like impressions that form in your mind. It's important to remain passive, let the visions flow to you, and resist the urge to actively search for meaning. Patience and practice are key here, as the art of scrying can take time to develop.

Interpreting Your Visions: The images seen during scrying are deeply personal and often symbolic. You might see literal images relating to past, present, or future events, or you might see symbolic representations of people, situations, or challenges. It's essential to trust your intuition when it comes to interpreting these visions. You may also find it helpful to keep a journal of your scrying sessions to track patterns, symbols, and their potential meanings.

Scrying in Modern Magic: In modern white magic practice, scrying continues to be a popular form of divination. It's a profound meditative practice that not only supports divinatory insight but also fosters self-reflection and growth. As you connect deeply with your subconscious and the energies of the universe, scrying can be an enriching tool on your spiritual journey.

Tea Leaf Reading (Tasseography)

Tasseography, or tea leaf reading, is an ancient and respected tradition within the realm of white magic. It's a form of divination that involves interpreting the patterns left by tea leaves in a cup after drinking. Rich with symbolic meaning and intuitive insight, this practice is a gentle and engaging way to explore the unseen threads of the universe that connect us all.

Tasseography originates from a time when omens in nature were seen as divine messages. Over centuries, this practice has evolved and taken on a refined structure, while still retaining its central belief in the meaningful patterns of the natural world.

Reading tea leaves is a contemplative, almost meditative practice. It begins with the preparation and consumption of a cup of loose-leaf tea, typically in a white or light-colored cup to see the leaves more clearly. It's during this calm and mindful tea-drinking ritual that your focused intention can open the door to intuitive insights.

Steps to Reading Tea Leaves:

1. Choosing Your Tea: Any loose-leaf tea can be used for reading, but small-leaf teas often work best as they create distinct shapes. It's best to avoid using a tea strainer, allowing the leaves to float freely.

2. Drinking the Tea: As you drink, focus your thoughts on the question or issue you're seeking insight into. This can be specific or general, depending on your needs.

3. Reading the Leaves: Once most of the liquid is gone, swirl the remaining tea around the cup three times and then invert the cup onto a saucer to drain the remaining tea. The leaves will be left clinging to the cup in a variety of patterns.

Interpreting Your Reading: The remaining tea leaves are read based on their placement and the images they form. The rim of the cup represents the present or near future, while the bottom symbolizes the distant future. The handle of the cup represents the person drinking the tea, and the leaves near the handle often relate to personal experiences.

Interpreting the symbols formed by the tea leaves is where intuition and creativity play crucial roles. An anchor might signify stability, a heart could symbolize love, and a bird may represent a journey or freedom. There are many traditional symbol interpretations, but your personal connection to a symbol is equally important.

Rune Casting

Rune casting, a revered and ancient form of divination, is deeply woven into the fabric of white magic. Originating from the Norse and Germanic cultures, the Runes carry a wealth of symbolic and spiritual significance. They are not merely a tool for divination, but a key to ancient wisdom and universal truths.

Runes are letters in a set of related alphabets known as runic alphabets, which were used to write various Germanic languages before the adoption of the Latin alphabet. However, in the context of magic and divination, each rune symbolizes more than just a phonetic sound. They represent complex concepts and archetypal energies. In essence, runes are a symbolic language, each character holding a universe of meanings.

The most commonly used runic alphabet in divination is the Elder Futhark, which consists of 24 characters. Each character or rune symbolizes a specific energy or concept, ranging from elements of nature like water (Laguz) and ice (Isa), to abstract notions such as joy (Wunjo) and chaos (Hagalaz).

Principles of Rune Casting: Rune casting, also known as rune reading, involves casting these runes and interpreting the resulting patterns to seek answers or gain insights. It's essential to approach rune casting with respect and mindfulness, understanding that you're engaging with a profound spiritual tradition.

In white magic, rune casting is performed with a clear and focused intention. The practitioner often begins by formulating a question or defining an area of guidance needed. Then, they would reach into a bag containing the runes, pull out a certain number, and cast them onto a cloth or table. The runes can be read based on their position, orientation, and their relation to the runes nearby.

Interpreting the Runes: Interpreting runes requires not only an understanding of the traditional meanings of each symbol but also intuition and personal insight. The same rune might whisper different messages in different contexts.

For example, the rune Ehwaz, symbolizing partnership and trust, might suggest cooperation in a business reading, the strengthening of a romantic relationship in a love reading, or the need to trust oneself in a personal growth reading.

Some runes have different meanings when they appear in reverse, similar to tarot cards. The practitioner needs to consider this when reading the runes.

I Ching

The I Ching, also known as the "Book of Changes," is an ancient Chinese divination text and a significant cornerstone in Eastern philosophy. Predating Confucianism and Taoism, it has deeply influenced these philosophies and remains a fundamental tool in understanding the principles of balance and change. In the context of white magic, the I Ching is a beautiful and intricate system that invites introspection and provides profound wisdom, allowing one to navigate through life's complexities with greater clarity and tranquility.

The I Ching's roots stretch back over three thousand years, making it one of the oldest divination systems in existence. At its core, the I Ching reflects the belief in the dynamic balance of opposites and the cyclical nature of events and situations. This belief manifests in the I Ching's primary symbols - Yin (representing passive, receptive force) and Yang (representing active, creative force).

Structure of I Ching: The I Ching employs 64 hexagrams, each comprised of six lines that are either broken (Yin) or unbroken (Yang). Each hexagram carries its unique meaning and interpretation, reflecting various states of change and equilibrium. These hexagrams are further broken down into eight 'trigrams' - groups of three lines - that represent elements of nature and aspects of human experience.

Practicing I Ching Divination: The divination process with the I Ching is often performed with three coins, each assigned a numerical value. You would throw the coins six times, recording the resulting total value for each throw. Each throw corresponds to a line, beginning from the bottom of your hexagram and moving upwards.

Based on the values you've recorded, you would construct a hexagram, interpreting the guidance of the I Ching based on this hexagram. To deepen the process, each line in the hexagram is also considered, offering specific advice or insights that further clarify the hexagram's overall message.

Dream Interpretation and Magic

The land of dreams has long been recognized as a realm of profound wisdom and insight. This mystical landscape where our consciousness roams freely while our physical bodies rest is an integral part of the human experience. In the context of white magic, dreams become even more significant, serving as an intersection where the physical world meets the spiritual, and our inner selves can communicate with the universe at large.

The Language of the Subconscious

Dreams are the language of the subconscious mind. They reflect our deepest fears, desires, experiences, and potential. Interpreting dreams is akin to deciphering a cryptic language, a mystical cipher in which each symbol, character, and landscape is loaded with multiple meanings. A successful dream interpretation can uncover hidden truths, provide guidance, and offer unique insights about the self and the path one is walking.

In white magic, dream interpretation goes a step further. It's not just about understanding our subconscious mind; it's about perceiving the messages from the divine or the universe. Practitioners of white magic believe that dreams can serve as warnings, reveal future events, or even provide solutions to current problems.

Moreover, dreams can facilitate contact with spiritual entities, guides, or departed loved ones. They are also a fertile ground for astral travel and other out-of-body experiences, all of which can have profound implications on a person's magical practice.

Working with Dreams in Your Practice

To saddle the control of dreams in your enchanted hone, begin by making dream work a portion of your schedule. Keep a dream diary by your bedside and record your dreams as before long as you wake up. As you relate your dreams, pay consideration to your feelings, considerations, and any images that stand out.

Interpretation is a highly personal process, as each symbol may carry a different meaning depending on the dreamer's cultural background, personal experiences, and current circumstances. Therefore, trust your intuition when deciphering your dreams. You may also wish to consult dream dictionaries or guides, but remember that the most accurate interpretation will always resonate with your intuition.

Enhancing Dream Work with White Magic

White magic can also be used to enhance your dream work. Here are a few techniques:

Dream Recall Spells: Recalling dreams can be difficult for many people as dreams are often elusive, fading away just as we wake up. However, there is a belief in certain magical practices that performing a dream recall spell can enhance our ability to remember these nightly narratives. A simple dream recall spell could be a phrase or incantation spoken with intent before falling asleep, something like "May I remember my dreams when I awaken." An elaborate version of a dream recall spell might involve creating a ritual space with calming candlelight, burning incense or sage, and positioning crystals and herbs around you. Amethyst is often used in these rituals as it is believed to have properties that aid in remembering dreams, and mugwort, a common herb in magical practices, is said to help open up the mind and enhance the clarity of dreams.

Focusing your intent and energy on remembering your dreams while performing the spell can increase the likelihood of success.

Dream Protection Spells: Dreams can be influenced by a variety of factors, and some may believe that negative influences or energies can affect our dreams. Dream protection spells aim to safeguard the dreamer, ensuring a peaceful and safe dream experience. A simple dream protection spell might involve placing a protective crystal, like black tourmaline, under your pillow before going to sleep. Black tourmaline is traditionally believed to ward off negative energy and create a barrier between you and any potential harm. A more elaborate dream protection spell could involve creating a protective circle around your sleeping area using a combination of salt, herbs, or even specific words of power spoken aloud. This circle serves as a protective boundary that wards off negative influences and energies, allowing you to have a safe and positive dream journey.

Lucid Dreaming Techniques: Clear envisioning alludes to the encounter of getting to be mindful that you're envisioning whereas you're still within the dream state. This awareness inside the dream can permit you to associated with and control your dream world, frequently driving to significant experiences and individual development. Strategies to advance clear envisioning can be as straightforward as practicing contemplation and certifications some time recently rest, centering on the purposeful to recognize and control your dreams. You'll moreover keep up a dream journal, where you type in down each detail of your dreams that you simply can review, which might increment your mindfulness and capacity to realize when you're in a dream. Another common strategy is the utilize of particular stones, like labradorite, a gem accepted to upgrade the association between our physical and ethereal or dream selves. Normal utilize of these procedures can increment the probability of clear envisioning, including a profitable instrument to your mysterious hone.

Astral Travel and Ethereal Work

In the mysterious and all-encompassing universe of white magic, there are myriad ways to explore the cosmos, our consciousness, and the invisible threads that connect every living being. Astral travel and ethereal work are two such practices that hold tremendous potential for transformation and spiritual growth.

Astral Travel

The astral plane, as perceived in theosophy and spiritual disciplines, is a trans-dimensional domain that exists beyond our physical universe. It's considered a dwelling for spirits, spiritual guides, and other ethereal entities. The laws of time and space as we perceive them may not necessarily be applicable here, providing the astral explorer with the ability to journey into the past, present, or future, visit diverse places, or interact with spiritual beings.

In the practice of benign or 'white' magic, the astral plane is also regarded as a dimension where significant learning and spiritual development can happen. It is a space where divine guidance can be sought, arcane wisdom gathered, and firsthand experience of the soul's existence can be gained.

Astral projection is typically brought about through deep meditation, setting intentions, and visualization. The process usually necessitates the practitioner reaching a state of deep relaxation, followed by a visualization of the astral body separating from the physical body.

Here is a simplified, sequential guide to commence practicing astral travel:

Relaxation: The first step in any meditative or introspective practice, such as astral projection, is achieving a state of deep relaxation. This process involves both physical and mental preparation. Start by finding a quiet, peaceful location where you're unlikely to be interrupted. Comfort is key, so ensure that you're in a position (such as lying down) that you can maintain for an extended period without discomfort. Now, close your eyes and turn your focus inwards. Concentrate on your breath, allowing your inhales and exhales to flow naturally and rhythmically. Acknowledge any thoughts that arise but let them drift away without engaging. With every breath, feel your body becoming more relaxed and your mind more peaceful. You might imagine a wave of relaxation flowing down your body, easing each muscle from your head to your toes. This step may take some time, particularly if you're new to these practices, but patience and persistence are key.

Mind Awake, Body Asleep: Often described as the hypnagogic state, this phase is an intermediary stage between being awake and sleeping that you may have encountered while falling asleep or upon waking up. The objective in this state is to retain mental awareness while your body enters a sleep-like condition. It's a fine equilibrium that demands practice. Your body should feel weighty, relaxed, and still, while your mind stays conscious and vigilant. You might start observing hypnagogic imagery—intense, dreamlike visuals or sounds that emerge as you get closer to sleep. It's crucial to simply watch these occurrences without responding or getting overly absorbed. Remain the aware observer, preserving your cognitive alertness while your body "falls asleep."

Vibrational Stage: As you delve deeper into this practice, you may start to feel what's typically known as the vibrational stage. This is generally identified by a feeling of resonance, buzzing, or humming all over your body. These sensations are believed to signify a transition in your consciousness and a preparation for astral travel. The intensity of these sensations can significantly differ and sometimes might be strong or mildly discomforting, but it's vital not to panic. If you stay peaceful and grounded, these vibrations can serve as a portal to the astral plane. It's essential to let the vibrations happen naturally, without attempting to manipulate or force them. They can imply that you're on the brink of an astral projection experience and are prepared to separate your astral body from your physical one. It's at this juncture that you can begin applying specific methods for initiating astral projection, such as the rope method, the roll-out technique, or the lift-out approach.

Separation: Once you've attained the vibrational stage and are entirely at ease with your mind alert, it's the moment to disengage your astral body from your physical form. This disconnection is a critical aspect of astral projection, with several techniques available to aid this process. One of the most commonly used methods is the 'rope strategy', which entails visualizing a rope dangling above you and utilizing it to draw your astral body out from your physical one. Envision extending your astral hands, grasping the rope, and hoisting yourself up, feeling the sensation of gently ascending and drifting away. Bear in mind, you're not aiming to physically move; all of this is occurring in your mind. Some individuals might feel a minor jolt or 'pop' as their astral body disengages, whereas others might perceive it as a soft and seamless procedure.

Astral Journey: Once you've successfully separated, you're at liberty to start your astral journey. Astral projection empowers you to explore the physical world and the astral plane from a fresh perspective. You may decide to just scrutinize your surroundings or adventure further, potentially visiting remote locations or even alternate dimensions. Some practitioners pursue interactions with spiritual beings or guides, aiming to acquire wisdom, insights, or help. Remember, while astral projection can be a thrilling and deep experience, it's crucial to approach it with respect and a sincere aspiration for understanding and development.

Reentry: Following your astral voyage, it's vital to come back to your physical body safely and effortlessly. To initiate this procedure, direct your thoughts towards your physical body and your intention to return. Typically, astral projection practitioners believe in a 'silver cord'—an energetic connection between the astral and physical bodies, ensuring you can always navigate your way back. By focusing on this cord, you can trace it back to your body. The return should be a tranquil process, and you might feel a sense of sliding back into your physical body. After your return, allocate a brief period to center yourself. It could be beneficial to move your fingers and toes, perform some stretches, and inhale deeply to prepare yourself for complete alertness. Dedicate some moments to contemplate your voyage and any significant realizations or encounters you encountered prior to resuming your daily routines.

Safety and Ethical Considerations: As with all practices in white magic, astral travel should be approached with respect, positive intention, and ethical consideration. Before undertaking an astral journey, it's wise to perform a protection ritual or spell. Call upon your guides or use protective symbols to ensure a safe journey.

During astral travel, practitioners are urged to respect the entities they may encounter and avoid any actions that could cause harm. White magic upholds the principle of 'do no harm', which should be adhered to during astral travel, just as in the physical world.

High Magic: Working with Deities and Higher Beings

The realm of high magic, often called ceremonial or ritual magic, is a deeply profound aspect of white magic practice. It invites us to connect with powerful spiritual entities, such as deities, angels, and spirit guides, harnessing their energy and wisdom to bring about transformative changes.

High magic is primarily concerned with spiritual growth, divine wisdom, and connection with the divine or the higher self. This realm of magic frequently entails intricate ceremonies, thorough groundwork, and a profound comprehension of symbolic frameworks like Qabalah, astrology, or the tarot. Within this context, our aim is to harmonize with divine forces and energies, with the intention of influencing transformation in both our personal lives and the world that surrounds us.

Working with Deities

Deities are powerful divine beings revered in various spiritual traditions. They represent different aspects of life, nature, and the universe, each carrying unique wisdom and power. Engaging with deities involves recognizing their presence, demonstrating reverence, and establishing a connection built on mutual understanding and confidence.

Selecting a Deity: The process of choosing a deity to establish a connection with is deeply personal, and there are numerous approaches to making this decision. One might feel a natural inclination towards a deity from their cultural heritage, perhaps a god or goddess from the ancestral pantheon. Another person might choose a deity based on their spiritual or philosophical beliefs. For example, a person drawn to nature might resonate with Gaia, the ancient Greek goddess of Earth. Personal inclination also plays a significant role – you may just feel a natural affinity towards a particular deity. Lastly, many practitioners select a deity according to the specific aspects, powers, or domains they govern. If your objective is to attain wisdom, one option could be selecting Athena, the Greek goddess known for her association with wisdom. Conversely, if your emphasis is on love and relationships, Aphrodite, the goddess of love, may be a suitable choice. Allocate sufficient time to explore and appreciate various deities, and rely on your inner guidance to direct you towards the deity that aligns with your intentions.

Establishing a Connection: Building a relationship with a deity takes time, sincerity, and respect. Start by learning as much as you can about the deity – their stories, attributes, symbols, and preferences. With this understanding, you can employ your knowledge to establish a connection with the chosen deity through practices such as prayer, meditation, or ritual. Prayer serves as a direct means of communicating with a deity, enabling you to convey your respect, express gratitude, or make specific requests. Meditation helps you quiet your mind and open yourself to any messages or guidance the deity may wish to impart. Rituals are another potent way to establish a connection, and they often involve offerings or sacrifices that are meaningful to the deity. It can also be beneficial to create a dedicated altar. This serves as a physical focus point for your relationship with the deity and can be adorned with their symbols, representations, and offerings. Regular engagement with this altar can deepen your connection with the deity.

Invoking a Deity: Invocation is a powerful practice within many spiritual traditions. Once you've established a connection with a deity, you can invite them to participate more directly in your spiritual or magical work by invoking their presence. An invocation is a call to the deity, a request for their energy, guidance, or assistance. This can be done through a formal ritual, a heartfelt prayer, or a simple spoken request. The key to successful invocation is a sincere intention, a respectful attitude, and a clear purpose. It's important to understand that invocation is not about controlling or demanding the deity but about inviting their influence and embodying their energy in your work. Remember to express gratitude and offer something in return for their help, such as an offering or service that aligns with the deity's values or domains.

Working with Higher Beings

Beyond deities, there are other higher beings that white magic practitioners often work with, such as angels, spirit guides, and ancestors.

Angels: Angels are perceived as divine messengers and protectors in many religious and spiritual traditions. They're believed to exist in a higher vibrational plane and are often associated with pure, positive energy. As celestial beings, they can be invoked for a variety of purposes. For instance, if you're seeking protection, you might call upon Archangel Michael, known for his protective qualities. For guidance and wisdom, Archangel Raphael is a common choice. When calling upon angels, it's important to be clear and respectful with your intentions. They can provide support and comfort in difficult times, lend their strength for healing, or offer insights to foster your spiritual growth. However, remember to show gratitude for their assistance and to listen with an open heart for their guidance.

Spirit Guides: Spirit guides are considered spiritual entities that provide guidance, support, and teaching throughout one's spiritual journey. Unlike angels, spirit guides can take numerous forms and often have a more personal connection to the individual they're assisting. They can be ancestral spirits, animal spirits, nature spirits, or ascended masters. Your spirit guides have chosen to be with you and help you navigate through your life's challenges. They offer wisdom, guidance, and sometimes even protection. To connect with your spirit guide, you might use meditation, journeying, or dream work. Always approach your spirit guides with respect, and remember to thank them for their guidance and support.

Ancestors: Honoring your ancestors is a central practice in many spiritual traditions. Your forebears possess a profound potential to provide guidance, wisdom, and spiritual strength. Having traversed their own challenges and adversities, their experiences can offer precious insights for your own path in life. To establish a connection with your ancestors, you can consider crafting an ancestor altar embellished with photographs, heirlooms, or other objects that evoke their memory. You can also dedicate rituals, make offerings, or simply take a moment each day to remember and honor them. Incorporating ancestral veneration into your practice can create a powerful link between you, your roots, and the spiritual realm, providing a strong foundation for your magical work.

Working with higher beings is not a practice to be taken lightly. Always approach them with utmost respect and reverence. Remember, they are not servants to command, but wise and powerful entities willing to assist those who approach them with a humble heart and a sincere intention.

Also, working with high magic often involves intense energies. Ensure that you are grounded, protected, and well-prepared before engaging in such practices. Always adhere to the ethical principles of white magic, namely respect for free will, do no harm, and responsibility for your actions.

Afterword: White Magic in Your Daily Life

White magic, at its essence, extends beyond being merely a collection of spells and rituals. It encompasses a way of life and a philosophy that transcends the confines of magical practices, permeating every aspect of our existence. It involves aligning ourselves with natural forces and the divine, fostering a profound reverence for all living beings and the world around us, and harnessing our inherent power to effect positive transformation.

The key to integrating magic into daily life lies in nurturing mindfulness. This entails consciously acknowledging and honoring the magic that permeates our being and surroundings. From the life-sustaining rays of the sun to the emotional influence of the moon's phases, magic surrounds us both internally and externally. Cultivate mindfulness by spending time in nature, practicing meditation, and consciously connecting with the universal energies.

A sacred space extends beyond traditional altars or temples. It can be any place where you infuse spiritual significance, feeling a deep connection with the divine and inner peace. This could be your garden, kitchen, or even your workspace. Fill these spaces with symbols, images, or objects that resonate with your spiritual beliefs, fostering a connection to the realm of magic.

Regularly purify yourself and your surroundings of negative energies. This can be achieved through smudging, engaging in a cleansing ritual bath, or employing visualization techniques for energy cleansing. Additionally, develop a habit of shielding yourself before leaving your home or when encountering negative situations or individuals.

Infuse magic into your meals by using ingredients with magical properties and imbuing your food and drinks with your intentions. For example, you could brew a tea with herbs that promote love and tranquility, or cook a meal using ingredients that attract abundance. Bless your food, thank the spirits of the plants and animals, and eat mindfully.

Rituals don't always have to be elaborate. They can be simple acts done with intent and reverence. This could be lighting a candle, saying a prayer, offering gratitude to the divine, or drawing a sigil. You can also align your rituals with the cycles of the moon, the changing seasons, or your personal routine.

Carry protective amulets, wear jewelry with specific stones that align with your intentions, or draw sigils on your body or belongings. These serve as reminders of your magical intentions and help you carry your magic with you throughout the day.

Tune in to the lunar cycle. Each phase of the moon carries different energies that can support your intentions and activities. For example, start new projects during the waxing moon, release what no longer serves you during the waning moon, and charge your magical tools under the full moon.

Community or Solitary Practice?

Just as in every spiritual path, the practice of white magic can be a communal or solitary endeavor. The companionship found in a community of like-minded individuals can provide a nurturing, supportive, and enriching environment for learning and growth. On the other hand, solitary practice allows for personal freedom and independence in shaping your unique magical path. This chapter explores the concepts of covens, groups, and solitary practice in the context of white magic.

Covens

A coven refers to a gathering of witches, generally ranging from three to thirteen members, who unite for spellcasting, celebrating sabbats and esbats, and providing mutual support. Despite its portrayal in popular culture, which may seem intimidating to some, a coven is fundamentally a spiritual family united by shared beliefs and rituals. A coven is typically headed by a High Priestess or High Priest and may adhere to a particular tradition or set of ceremonies.

Being part of a coven can deliver a feeling of community and provide a forum for the exchange of experiences, knowledge, and energy. Covens can serve as educational spaces, where seasoned witches mentor those with less experience. They offer a framework that many practitioners find reassuring and beneficial.

However, it's vital to understand that becoming a coven member requires dedication. This commitment includes participation in group ceremonies, attendance at gatherings, contributions to the coven, and in some cases, compliance with particular codes or traditions. This level of commitment or structured approach may not align with every practitioner's preferences.

Groups

Apart from formal covens, there are also less structured groups that people can join. These can be study groups, circles for celebrating sabbats, online communities, or local meet-ups. Such groups often allow for more flexibility than covens, both in terms of commitment and practices.

Groups can be a wonderful opportunity for those who wish to share and learn from others, but prefer a less rigid structure than a coven. They can offer a sense of community and companionship without the same level of obligation.

Solitary Practice

Many practitioners of white magic are solitary witches, choosing to practice their craft alone. This does not mean they are isolated or without community; many solitary witches maintain connections with other practitioners, join online communities, or participate in public pagan events.

Solo practice offers total independence in crafting one's spiritual journey. A solitary witch has the liberty to formulate their own beliefs, rites, and practices without needing to conform to a collective consensus. While this route can be profoundly personal and rewarding, it also necessitates self-drive, discipline, and the capacity to tackle obstacles independently.

The choice to practice within a coven, a group, or alone is a deeply individual decision. Each modality has its unique advantages and difficulties. You may prefer one over the others, or you may transition among them at various phases of your path. The crucial factor is to select the approach that best aligns with you and allows you to evolve and manifest your magical practice in the most genuine and satisfying manner. Remember, in white magic, there's no single 'correct' way to be a practitioner - only the method that suits you best.

Personal Growth and Spiritual Development Through Magic

At its essence, white magic embodies harmony, healing, and growth. It is not just about performing spells to induce desired alterations in the physical realm; it also concerns personal advancement and spiritual maturation. When perceived in this context, the practice of white magic evolves into a transformative journey of self-exploration, healing, and self-sufficiency.

One of the wonderful facets of practicing white magic is the self-exploration journey it facilitates. As you educate yourself about the universal energies around you, you simultaneously learn about the energies within you. You start understanding your strengths, weaknesses, passions, and fears. You reveal your spiritual talents and capabilities, discovering the divine spark dwelling within you.

Participation in rituals, meditation, divination, and other magical practices can expose your concealed aspects, both light and shadow. These practices promote introspection, aiding you in comprehending your profound desires, motivations, and life's purpose.

Arguably, one of the most powerful ways white magic contributes to personal development is through empowerment. By learning to channel and mold the energies of the universe, you become an active contributor to your reality's creation. You're no longer a passive bystander subject to fate. Instead, you understand that you possess the power to materialize your desires and influence your destiny.

Through spellcasting, you learn to concentrate your intent, visualize your objectives, and tap into your personal power to instigate change. This sense of empowerment can infiltrate all facets of your life, endowing you with confidence and a sense of purpose.

The practice of white magic is a spiritual pursuit. It is a path that encourages connection with the divine, however you perceive it - as a personal deity, a universal life force, the spiritual essence within all beings, or an entirely different concept.

Through rituals, meditation, and other practices, you can cultivate a profound, personal relationship with the divine. This spiritual bond can offer guidance, solace, and wisdom, and can assist you in managing life's trials with grace and resilience.

Furthermore, white magic fosters a feeling of unity with all of life. It instills a respect for nature and nurtures the recognition of the divine in all beings. This can lead to spiritual revelations and awakenings, infusing your life with a profound sense of meaning and purpose.

***

A As we conclude this exploration of the world of white magic, I hope that you've not only acquired a trove of knowledge but also a profound understanding of the intrinsic magic within you. This magic forms a part of your essence, your identity, and your life; it isn't separate from you but rather intertwined with your very existence.

With every spell you cast, every herb you employ, and each time you synchronize with the lunar cycle or align your chakras, you forge a deeper connection with this magic and, consequently, with yourself. The journey into white magic is a voyage of self-realization, personal development, and spiritual progress.

White magic embodies balance, harmony, and love. Utilize it to foster positive transformation in your life and in the lives of those around you. Continue to discover, educate yourself, and evolve in your practice, and always let your intuition, your heart, and your ethical values guide you.

Thank you for undertaking this path. May your journey in white magic be a wellspring of light, love, and profound wisdom. As you progress forward, may the magic forever be with you!

Made in the USA
Middletown, DE
25 August 2024

59723949R00080